Why Culture Counts

Teaching Children of Poverty

Donna Walker Tileston   Sandra K. Darling

Solution Tree | Press

a division of
Solution Tree

555 North Morton Street
Bloomington, IN 47404
800.733.6786 (toll free) / 812.336.7700
FAX: 812.336.7790
email: info@solution-tree.com
solution-tree.com

Cover art and design by Grannan Design, Ltd.

Printed in the United States of America

13 12 11 10 09   2 3 4 5

FSC
Mixed Sources
Product group from well-managed
forests and other controlled sources
Cert no. SW-COC-002283
www.fsc.org
© 1996 Forest Stewardship Council

ISBN 978-1-934009-24-6

To turnaround teachers everywhere who carry the flame of hope to children. To turnaround leaders Belinda Williams and Rosilyn Carroll, who ignited that flame and who have dedicated their lives to helping every child be successful.

—Donna Walker Tileston

To Chuck Lowry, for sharing his incredible passion and resources selflessly toward assuring that *all* children will learn.

—Sandra K. Darling

Acknowledgments

My thanks go out to all of the people at Solution Tree who believed in this project and who have cheered us on, including Ed Levy, our editor extraordinaire; Gretchen Knapp, our head cheerleader; and Jeff Jones, who believed in the project enough to put his staff behind us to see it through.

—Donna Walker Tileston

All of us stand on the shoulders of our teachers. They allow us to reach higher and see farther than we ever thought possible. This work would not have its power without my teachers. They taught me, believed in me, and inspired me to persist in attempting what I thought was impossible. Dr. Belinda Williams and Dr. Rosilyn Carroll continually—without judgment—challenged my thinking; Dr. Virginia Riser kept me ethically grounded; David Frost, a hero with the utmost integrity, provided encouragement during the darkest days; and finally, my mom and first teacher, Veronica Mesna, taught me to believe in myself and my mission in spite of overwhelming adversity.

—Sandra K. Darling

Table of Contents

About the Authors

Donna Walker Tileston, Ed.D., is the founder and president of Strategic Teaching and Learning in Dallas, Texas. She has presented at international, national, and state conferences to thousands of educators and has presented her research in Warsaw and The Hague. Donna is the author of 23 books including her bestselling series *What Every Teacher Should Know,* which won the Association of Educational Publisher's Distinguished Achievement Award in 2005. Donna's training and keynotes include "Why Culture Counts, 21st-Century Leaders: What's the Difference?" The *What Every Teacher Should Know* series is offered for graduate-level credits at California State University and Hamline University; many of her courses are also offered for alternative certification in various states. More information about Donna's writing, keynotes, and training can be found on her website, www.wetsk.com.

Sandra K. Darling, Ph.D., is the founder and president of Learning Bridges. Grounded in 5 years of research, the Learning Bridges Aligned Instructional Database contains the most effective, research-based instructional strategies for the standards of all states—in order of their impact on learning. Born into extreme poverty in rural Minnesota, Sandra understands the power of having significant adults in her life who believed in her, had high expectations for her, and taught her the value of integrity. She has coauthored three books, published articles in several education journals, and presented to thousands of educators on standards-based education, curriculum alignment, inclusion practices, transformational leadership, school improvement, strategic planning, and assessment practices. She is a leading expert on aligning instructional strategies to content standards and delivering that instruction with the modifications needed to close the gap in achievement for students from poverty, diverse cultures, and English-language learners.

Foreword

By Belinda Williams

"I thought Oz was a great Head," said Dorothy. . . . "No; you are all wrong," said the little man, meekly. "I have been making believe." "Making believe!" cried Dorothy. "Are you not a great Wizard?" "Hush, my dear," he said. "Don't speak so loud, or you will be overheard—and I should be ruined. I'm supposed to be a Great Wizard."

—L. Frank Baum, *The Wizard of Oz*

By most accounts, the belief in "a great Head"—the promise that standards, testing, and accountability in and of themselves would impact academic achievement gaps—has failed terribly (Bracey, 2006). In the introduction to L. Frank Baum's classic children's tale, *The Wizard of Oz,* Baum describes the fairy tale as one in which "the wonderment and joy are retained and the heart-aches and nightmares are left out." Born out of *Brown vs. Board of Education,* Lyndon Johnson's War on Poverty, and the Title I Elementary and Secondary Education Act (ESEA, 1965), No Child Left Behind is the most clearly defined federal education policy. It proposes *simplicity*—that is, standards, testing, and accountability—to close achievement gaps between the identified subgroups and white middle-class students. These enacted NCLB strategies leave out the "heart-aches and night-mares" and enable federal and state governments to avoid attention to the complex issues and underpinnings that contributed to the passage of ESEA, namely the historical and persistent racial, ethnic, cultural, and socioeconomic gaps chronicled by Jennings (2000).

Current criticisms of the federal policy range from the emphasis on assessment and arguments regarding the 1% rule (limiting the reporting of adequate yearly progress of special education students assessed by alternative achievement standards) to underfunding, accountability, and teacher qualifications. Whatever the import of these arguments, there remains unaddressed the requirement of paying attention to the complex underpinnings of historically evidenced achievement gaps among African American, Asian, Native American, Mexican American, Latino, and socioeconomically disadvantaged students, as well as English-language learners—that is, the social, political, and economic experiences, beliefs, and expectations that each cultural group brings to the classroom.

Simplistic strategies for reform, including charters, vouchers, standards, class size reduction, decentralization, after-school and summer school programs, however challenging and expensive, will not work. Closing achievement gaps requires systemic change across the education community (federal and state governments, school districts, local communities, higher education, and so on) and cannot be accomplished without strengthening the ability of educators to address the challenges of attending to the "heart-aches and nightmares"—the complexities neither addressed by current policy nor elaborated by think tanks, associations, and agencies. To strengthen the abilities of educators, in *Why Culture Counts: Teaching Children of Poverty,* Tileston and Darling illuminate these complexities and introduce an *asset model* of instruction to address achievement gaps evidenced by students whose cultural experiences and poverty continue to be viewed as deficits.

A recent survey (Parsad, Lewis, & Farris, 2000) reveals that only 32% of teachers say they have the knowledge and skills to educate diverse populations of students. Absent the body of knowledge and skills required, the ability of educators across the country to interpret the nature of achievement gaps and address the distinct differences among group achievement patterns is left to chance. Students who are members of subgroups come to school with different experiences in cultures, values, priorities, and socioeconomic conditions. That must be understood if teachers are going to successfully engage them in the same standard curriculum (Cohen & Ball, 2001). In *Why Culture Counts: Teaching Children of Poverty,* the authors offer an instructional design to counter the assumptions of deficit interpretations of achievement gaps. The chapters describe differentiating instruction for context, content and product, process, and assessment. The descriptions and examples delineate how resilience and the strengths that students bring to school—their experiences, interests, knowledge, and so forth—provide rich opportunities to strengthen education programs and instructional strategies. Tileston and Darling move beyond problem identification to bring together research and theory that elaborate and integrate the three components of an instructional model (context, content and product, and process). Tileston and Darling also expand the repertoire of strategies educators use to differentiate instruction for students who are culturally diverse and living in poverty.

This volume provides an opportunity for the education community to move outside of old paradigms, limited by deficit assumptions and narrowly defined reform proposals and solutions, to fully engage populations of students that the education system has historically failed. *Why Culture Counts: Teaching Children of Poverty* contains important understandings of learning and instruction and will make a significant contribution to the education community, and to the lives of culturally diverse and socioeconomically disadvantaged students.

Belinda Williams, Psy.D., *is a cognitive psychologist and the editor of* Closing the Achievement Gap: A Vision for Changing Beliefs and Practices.

References

Bracey, G. W. (2006). The 16th Bracey Report on the condition of public education. *Phi Delta Kappan, 88*(2), 151–166.

Cohen, D. K., & Ball, D. L. (2001). Making change: Instruction and its improvement. *Phi Delta Kappan, 83*(1), 73–77.

Jennings, J. F. (2000). Title I: Its legislative history and its promise. *Phi Delta Kappan, 81*(7), 516–522.

Parsad, B., Lewis, L., & Farris, E. (2000). Teacher preparation and professional development: 2000. *Education Statistics Quarterly, 3*(3).

Introduction

Few Americans realize that the U.S. educational system is one of the most unequal in the industrialized world, and students routinely receive dramatically different learning opportunities based on their social status. In contrast to most European and Asian nations that fund schools centrally and equally, the wealthiest 10 percent of school districts in the United States spend nearly ten times more than the poorest 10 percent, and spending ratios of three to one are common within states. Poor and minority students are concentrated in the less well-funded schools, most of them located in central cities and funded at levels substantially below those of neighboring suburban districts.

—Linda Darling-Hammond and Laura Post

We have written this book for the 35 million and counting who live in poverty in the United States alone. We have written this book for all those children who go to school undernourished; who don't have the means to buy mittens to wear on a cold morning; who, because of where they were born, may not have the same vocabulary skills as the middle-class children in their classrooms; who may enter kindergarten already significantly behind them in background knowledge, vocabulary, and experience, resulting in a gap in achievement even before they begin. We have written this book because we think inequality in education is shameful in a country that is abundantly wealthy. While the United States Supreme Court made equal access the law of the land in *Brown v. Board of Education,* it did not make equal access to *quality* the law of the land. We think it is time to change unequal quality in education for good. As teachers, we have the power to do that more than any other group. And when we do, we don't just change education. We change communities, we change the quality of life for all of us, and we strengthen the weakening middle class.

Both of us have lived in poverty, and both of us have extensive experience working with children and teens who live in poverty, but we did not write this book from personal experience. We based it on hard evidence and extensive research into the strategies that truly make a difference in student learning for diverse learners— for students living in poverty, students from diverse cultures, and students new to the United States, especially those from the African American and Mexican American communities.

In chapter 1, we provide the most current data about poverty and the power of culture. We explain why we are presenting not a deficit model but a model that values the assets children bring to the classroom. We will introduce the steps of a new differentiation model that accomplishes two educational goals simultaneously: improving achievement *and* closing the gap for diverse learners.

Chapter 2 provides the rationale for an innovative differentiation process and an overview of its components. Here we introduce a research-based model for children living in poverty and from diverse cultures based on four steps:

1. Building teacher background knowledge

2. Planning to differentiate

3. Differentiating instructional delivery

4. Differentiating assessment

In sum, this chapter describes a model that provides research-based information that is immediately usable in the classroom.

How do we become "turnaround teachers" who provide intervention strategies to students at every age and grade level? And what do those intervention strategies look like?

In chapters 3 through 7, we look at each of the steps of our model in turn. Chapter 3 discusses the key ideas necessary to shift our beliefs and instructional practice and also discusses the critical background knowledge needed by teachers. Here, we assist educators in comprehending the significance of the distinction between collectivist and individualist value systems. We show the power of vocabulary to increase achievement and build background knowledge. We provide the rationale for creating culturally responsive classrooms in order to close achievement gaps. And we explain what educators need to do in diverse classrooms to promote a no-excuses approach to holding high expectations so that all children can succeed.

In chapter 4, we introduce the components to consider when planning to differentiate to meet the needs of children of poverty and diverse cultures. We explore examples from both elementary and secondary classrooms that incorporate planning to preteach vocabulary, contextualize content and the classroom environment for culture, modify effective instruction, and plan to provide opportunities for students to work together.

In chapters 5, 6, and 7, we show how to differentiate instructional delivery. We do this in three parts. Chapter 5 discusses the first way to differentiate instruction: for context. We address what effective teachers in a culturally responsive classroom are like and what they do. We explain how to create a culturally responsive classroom, and we furnish two examples—one for African American students and one for Mexican American students—so that you can see what differentiation looks like for the two largest minority cultures represented in American schools. Finally, we provide research-based and culturally responsive instructional strategies that teachers can use immediately.

Chapter 6 discusses the second way to differentiate instruction: for content and product. What kinds of products do we want our students to be able to create? What levels do we expect them to accomplish? How can we ensure that all children are getting the quality education they deserve and that all children can work at a quality level? We answer these questions by attending to the three *r*'s: relevance, rigor, and relationships (with a particular focus on relevance). We will not leave any room for shoddy or unfinished work or for anything below what our students can do. Chapter 6 also examines the classroom for bias and incorporates ideas for content that are relevant to the experiences of all learners. The ways in which students demonstrate their learning—student products—can also be differentiated to meet the needs of diverse learners, and we will provide specific examples on ways to accomplish this.

In chapter 7 we show the final way we differentiate instruction: through process. Here we discuss the most effective ways to assist students in creating personal meaning in the content or standards you are teaching in the classroom. We tie process to the systems of thinking, through which all learning tasks are processed by the brain. Again, we provide highly effective, research-based instructional strategies to accomplish this, drawn from the Learning Bridges Aligned Instructional Database.

In chapter 8, we share ways in which assessment can be differentiated to assist diverse learners in demonstrating what they know and can do. We discuss the purpose of various types of assessments and how their results are used in education. And we provide specific guidelines to support teachers in choosing that are appropriate to their content, that will inform their teaching, and that will assist diverse learners in showing what they've learned.

Chapter 9 puts all the pieces together to show how to build resilience in diverse learners and children of poverty. We provide two approaches for teachers to immediately begin their own work in differentiating instruction for these learners.

This book was a labor of love, a love for children everywhere but in particular those children for whom the American dream has been elusive due to the status of their birth, the place they live, or the kind of access that has been afforded them. In one of our favorite poems, a young student in one of our classes long ago writes of painting a star on her window so that even on the cloudiest nights she could still make a wish.

We want to provide that star.

CHAPTER ONE

Culture and Poverty

We define culture as the systems of values, beliefs, and ways of knowing that guide communities of people in their daily lives.

—Elise Trumbull

As educators join forces with sociologists, behaviorists, and researchers, the question has become, "Is it culture or poverty that creates the discrepancies in achievement among groups that we find in the classroom today?" Studies indicate that it is not culture *or* poverty, but culture *and* poverty. A preponderance of evidence from these studies indicates that we need to look at culture first and then at the circumstances of children living in poverty. Why culture first? If we truly want to raise the learning levels of our students, we must first know the culture from which they come. We must know how that culture learns, the value it places on education, and how, within that culture, motivation is triggered. This does not mean teachers have to study every culture in North America; it means that as teachers we have to know the culture of the students in our schools and of the neighborhoods that surround them. We also need to stop focusing on the deficits and look at the gifts—the life experiences—that our students bring with them. When we know this, we can make more informed decisions about how to teach them.

Deficit Models Don't Work

Bonnie Benard (1996, 1997) defined the deficit model of differentiation in this way: "The cultural deficit perspective focuses educational discourse on the problems of school failure, the 'achievement gap,' and dropout rates" (p. 98). In the latter part of the 20th century, students coming from poverty were viewed based on their deficits. Education addressed the qualities and strengths that were lacking in these students, rather than looking at the gifts that they brought to the classroom. According to Belinda Williams (2003), social scientists and educators tended to look at cultural deficits and deprivation, researchers attempted to look for genetic inferiority, and state education agencies held up the failure of urban schools and urban educators. Low expectations led to an inferior curriculum and assessment program in many schools. The percentage of minority students in special education classes was often way out of proportion to the general population. Children of poverty who entered school with less vocabulary than their counterparts from middle and upper income brackets were often placed in pull-out programs because they were thought to have learning deficits, which may well have been simply a vocabulary difference.

Stephenson and Ellsworth (1993) concurred with this analysis:

> A common perception among both educators and the public is that students [fail and] drop out of school because of personal deficiencies or family or cultural deprivation. Contributing to this perception is a research and policy agenda, as well as professional and popular literature on school dropouts that have concentrated on the personal and demographic characteristics of dropouts themselves. The message, once again, is that students are the problem. This, in turn, implies that schools bear little responsibility for students dropping out and therefore can take few actions to reduce the number of dropouts. (p. 259)

A New Differentiation Model for Culture and Poverty

Throughout this book we present a new model for differentiation, based on hard evidence and scientifically based research about what will make a difference for students from poverty and diverse cultures. As we have seen, the model has four component parts: building background knowledge; planning; differentiating instructional delivery, with its core areas of context, content and product, and process; and differentiating assessment. Let's examine each of the core areas more closely.

Differentiating Context

Context speaks to the culture of the students. How do they learn best—individually or in groups? What world view do they bring from their culture, and what kind of classroom will best reflect that culture? What is the role of socialization in their culture? For example, in African American culture, relationships are essential before learning can take place. Therefore, a teacher in an African American classroom must build a relationship with her students first and provide the learning second. Bonnie Benard (1996, 2003) addresses relationships in the context of social competency, which is one of her keys for developing the resilience students need to achieve success in spite of the conditions of poverty and the differences in culture. She defines social competence this way:

> Social competence consists of relationship skills. It involves responsiveness, especially the ability to elicit positive responses from others; flexibility, including the ability to move back and forth between primary culture and dominant culture (cross-cultural competence); and empathy, caring, communication skills, and a sense of humor. (p. 99)

If we want to build this skill in our students from poverty, we must exhibit the skill ourselves as we work with them. Researchers often point to studies by Feuerstein (1980) showing that students who overcome adverse conditions can always point to a relationship from someone outside of their immediate circumstances who has provided a strong mentoring role. Studies by Rutter (1985) and Werner and Smith (1992) showed that at least half of children growing up in families where parents were mentally ill, alcoholic, abusive, or criminal, or in communities that were poverty-stricken or torn by war, actually *do* become competent, healthy, and successful adults. This is more likely to occur if, as children and youth, they experienced nurturing somewhere in their lives. These conditions are the context in which children live and learn.

Another aspect of the context in which children live as identified by Benard (1996) is "a sense of purpose and future." She defines it this way: "A sense of purpose and future signifies goal direction, educational aspirations, achievement motivation, persistence, hopefulness, optimism, and spiritual connectedness" (p. 99). Culture often dictates the attitude toward schools and learning that students bring with them. In a culture where poverty continues in spite of the fact that people attend school, people may in fact believe that education does not make a difference. If students believe that going to school makes no difference, they are more likely to be chronically absent, sleep in class, and not finish work. The cultural context in which students live has a great impact on what happens in our classrooms.

Differentiating Content and Product

The second core area of our model addresses the content to be learned and the products that students create in order to demonstrate their learning. How do we differentiate for content and knowledge acquisition? Benard (1996) addresses knowledge acquisition and content to be learned when discussing the fourth aspect of resiliency: problem-solving skills. She explains it this way:

> Problem-solving skills encompass the ability to plan; to be resourceful in seeking help from others; and to think critically, creatively, reflectively, and flexibly, trying out

alternate solutions to both cognitive and social problems. Other critical components of problem-solving are the development of a critical consciousness; an awareness of the structures of oppression (whether by an alcoholic parent, an insensitive school, or a racist society); and the creation of strategies for overcoming them. (p. 99)

As we explore modifications to content, to the activities we will engage our students in to learn, and to the products they will create to demonstrate that learning, we will be differentiating for content and product.

Differentiating Process

The third core area of the model speaks to the process of learning. What are the stages of the learning process? How do those stages interface with human development? How do children of poverty process information best? Which teaching methods are most effective? How do we get students to engage in the learning to make meaning for themselves? Benard (1996), in her research on resilience, refers to *autonomy* as one of the characteristics needed for children to engage in the learning process. People who have autonomy not only start a task, but they finish it at a quality level. They are able to complete processes. Benard identifies autonomy in this way:

Autonomy has to do with a sense of one's own identity. It involves an ability to act independently and to exert some control over one's environment, and it includes a sense of task mastery, internal locus of control, self-agency, and self-efficacy. The development of resistance (refusing to accept negative messages about oneself or one's culture and of detachment, distancing oneself from parental, school, or community dysfunction) serves as a powerful protector of autonomy. (p. 99)

If we want students to engage in the learning process successfully to make meaning of the content, we need to differentiate our instruction to attend to process.

This model was created to increase academic achievement *and* close the gaps between groups of students so that all can succeed in the classroom. While that is critically important, we believe that the model will also lead to the development of resilience, which is important beyond the classroom. Children who are resilient are able to successfully adapt despite risk and adversity (Maston, 1994; Garmezy, 1991; Hetherington, Cox, & Cox, 1982).

Poverty in America

When we think of poverty, we are more likely to think of images of starving children from third-world countries than of North America. Some of us may think, "Surely where there is so much abundance, people who live in poverty must do so by choice. If they would just get a job or get married, they would not be in poverty." In fact, bring up the issue of poverty, and you will get many strong opinions about whether it exists or not. But ask a teacher in a high-crime, inner-city neighborhood if poverty exists. Ask a teacher in a rural and poor farming community if poverty exists. Ask a teacher in an aging suburb, where the demographics and crime rates are changing, if poverty exists. They will tell you that it is very much alive and that children come to them malnourished and often with both physical and emotional health issues. They will tell you that the gap in education begins prior to walking in the door to kindergarten and first grade. They will tell you that for many children, the entrance to a first-grade classroom is across a gap rather than a threshold (Tileston, 2004a). They will tell you that children of poverty often start school with another gap—in vocabulary, the ability to plan, an understanding of cause and effect, and other prerequisite skills for academic achievement.

In his 2005 book, *One Nation, Underprivileged*, Rank says that the answer to why poverty exists in a country like the United States, amid all its abundance, "lies in the manner in which poverty has typically been viewed and acted on in the United States—that poverty is the result of individual inadequacies, that poverty lies outside the mainstream American experience, and therefore that poverty is not a national priority" (p. 6).

It should be noted that white children represent the largest *number* of children of poverty in the United States. However, children from other racial groups represent the largest *percentage* of children living in poverty for each racial group. According to the U.S. Census Bureau, as reported by Kunjufu (2006), the data regarding the 40 million who live below the poverty line break down as shown in Table 1-1.

Table 1-1: Poverty According to Racial and Ethnic Groups in the United States as of 2006

Cultural Group	Population in Poverty	Percentage of the Total U.S. Population in Poverty	Percentage of the Cultural Group Population in Poverty
White	20 million	50%	10%
African American	9 million	23%	25%
Hispanic	9 million	23%	25%
Asian or Native American	2 million	5%	16%

We often think about poverty in terms of African Americans, Hispanics, and Native Americans. Perhaps this is because from a percentage point of view, these ethnicities tend to be more concentrated. For example, according to Kunjufu (2006), "From an aggregate perspective, there are more whites below the poverty line than African Americans—20 million to 9 million. From a percentage perspective, 25% of African Americans live below the poverty line and only 10% of Whites" (p. 29). Kunjufu also points out that the African American population who live in poverty do so in densely populated urban areas, while poor whites tend to be more scattered in rural areas, mountain regions, trailer homes, and other types of housing.

Some Consequences of Poverty

Currently, the U.S. middle class is shrinking. While some people are gaining affluence, many more are losing ground and slipping downward toward poverty. Rank (2005) says, "Perhaps one of the most serious consequences of poverty, along with a disproportionate growth of wealth at the top, is the bifurcation of our society. We are increasingly becoming a society of haves and have nots" (p. 158). Rank cites abundant research showing that the gap between the poor and the affluent has been growing since the 1980s. All of us should be working to lift children of poverty so the next generation will have a strong middle class.

How Do We Define Poverty in Education?

As a general rule, American schools use the U.S. Census Bureau's charts to define poverty in a subgroup for their state tests and demographic reports. They also use the percentage of students who qualify to receive free or reduced-cost lunches in school, since in the United States, Title I federal funding uses that criterion. Schools are also compared using many measures, including the percentage of students in poverty or in a given low socioeconomic status as defined by the federal government.

Table 1-2 shows an example of how poverty is currently defined (Kunjufu, 2006). These definitions do not account for differences in the cost of living in various regions, or for the cost of healthcare. Instead, these are across-the-board levels of poverty. We all know that there is a marked difference in the cost of living between New York City and a small town in Iowa. Yet all areas are lumped together in determining socioeconomic status. In other words, the demographics in the United States—reported by schools in terms of socioeconomic status—may be only the tip of the iceberg in terms of who really is poor.

Table 1-2: Poverty Levels in the U.S. for 2006 by Size of Family Unit

Number of Persons in Family Unit	Forty-Eight Contiguous States and D.C.	Alaska	Hawaii
1	$ 9,800	$12,250	$11,270
2	$13,200	$16,500	$15,180
3	$16,600	$20,000	$19,090
4	$20,000	$25,000	$23,000
5	$23,400	$29,250	$26,910
For each additional person add:	$3,400	$4,250	$3,910

What the Data Say

From the literature we know the following:

- Poverty-prone children are more likely to be in single-parent families. Median female wages in the United States, at all levels of educational attainment, are 30% to 50% lower than male wages at the same level of educational attainment (Rank, 2005).

- Children under 6 remain particularly vulnerable to poverty. Those living in families with a female head of household and no husband present experienced a poverty rate of 50.3%, more than five times the rate for children in married-couple families, which was 9% (Rank, 2005).

- Within the African American community, one out of four men who reaches age 25 will have spent time in prison or on a suspended sentence, while three out of four of their white counterparts will have gone on to college (Rank, 2005, p. 159).

- Only 41% of African American male students in the regular education program graduate from high school (Kunjufu, 2005b).

- The mean reading score of a school's students can be predicted by the aggregated rates of childhood poverty and various epidemiological problems (Wang & Kovach, 1996).

- Children of poverty are more likely to contract lead poisoning, measles, and tuberculosis. McCord and Freeman (1990) reported that some U.S. inner-city neighborhoods had a lower life expectancy than some third-world countries. Since the time of their article, poverty rates have actually increased in the United States.

- Children of poverty are more likely to be crime victims, receive inadequate healthcare, and suffer from a wide variety of physical, psychological, and social problems (Wang & Kovach, 1996).

- According to an article by Blaine Harden in the *Washington Post* (Harden, 2006), middle-class neighborhoods, long regarded as incubators of the American dream, are losing ground in cities across the United States. Harden cited data from the Brookings Institution, based on a study from Wayne State University of 100 major cities and a selected group of 12 suburbs, showing that middle-income neighborhoods as a percentage of all metropolitan neighborhoods declined from 58% in 1970 to 41% in 2000 (Harden, 2006).

- Proficiency on reading scores for the five major ethnic groups in the United States indicate that adequate progress is not being met over time for those ethnic groups with the highest percentage of children in poverty; some have lost ground since 1992 (Kunjufu, 2006).

- Accompanying the decline of the manufacturing base of the U.S. economy and the economic restructuring of cities is an unprecedented increase in the number of children and families living in segregated and often highly adverse circumstances, placing those children at risk of school failure. The more a school draws its students from poor neighborhoods riddled with social problems, the worse its students perform academically (Wang & Kovach, 1996).

- Catherine Gewertz (2007) found that 44% of higher achieving lower-income children fall out of the top quartile in reading between the first and fifth grades, compared with 31% of high achievers whose family incomes are above the national median.

Educators have tried various approaches to helping students from poverty. Some have been a disaster. We know that programs that isolate minorities and children of poverty (for example, Title I and special education) have often added to the problem and may be based on preconceived ideas about these students.

Figure 1-1 from the U.S. Census Bureau (2006) shows the poverty rate increased for children less than 18 years old from roughly 14% in 1970 to 17.6% in 2005.

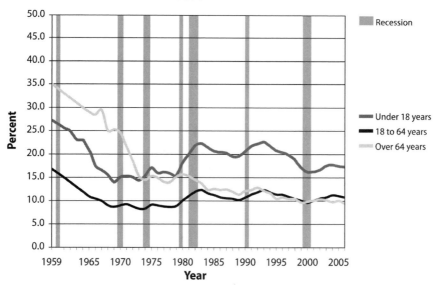

Figure 1-1: U.S. Census Bureau report on income, poverty, and insurance by age, from 1959–2005

Poverty affects us all. Those who wear blinders and believe that poverty is someone else's problem need to look around at the effects on society in terms of the economic, social, and psychological costs to each of us. As Rank (2005) says:

The issues that many Americans are in fact deeply concerned about, such as crime, access to and affordability
of healthcare, race relations, and worker productivity, to
name but a few, are directly affected and exacerbated by
the condition of poverty. As a result, the general public
winds up paying a heavy price for allowing poverty to
walk in our midst. (p. 110)

Poverty and Race

Early studies on poverty and its effects on education seemed to
indicate that the effects of poverty could be seen in all races equally.
Nothing could be further from the truth. New studies indicate that
besides poverty, culture plays an important part in many of the gaps
in education. In an article for *Education Week,* Catherine Gewertz
(2007) discussed a report from Civic Enterprises, a Washington-
based research and public-policy group, and the Jack Kent Cooke
Foundation, which coproduced the "Achievement Trap" study. Gewertz
says that these studies show that "higher achieving children from
lower-income families enter school with a disadvantage that shows
up in their national test sores. More than 70% of first graders who
score in the top quartile are from higher-income families, and fewer
than three in 10 are from lower-income families" (Gewertz, 2007).
The study shows that even those low-income students who score
well at grade 1 often lose ground in the time between the first and
fifth grades. There are racial gaps as well. The study shows that
lower-income Asian students, influenced by their culture, are more
likely to remain in the top quartile in math during high school than
their counterparts. African American students were the least likely
group to rise into that top tier in reading or math. Gewertz (2007)
quotes Michelle M. Fine, professor of social psychology and urban
education at the City University of New York, in a discussion of differences in academic achievement. She concludes that viewing the
success of lower income Asian kids tells us that more is at work than

socioeconomic status in test results, because these kids do well across the board.

In finding solutions, we must look at both culture and poverty so that we can utilize the experiences, beliefs, and expectations that each culture brings to the classroom and then differentiate based on both culture and poverty issues.

The Good News

As teachers, we have been given the responsibility to provide all children with a quality education and to prepare them for success on a global level. Thomas Friedman, in *The World Is Flat* (2005), points out that unskilled labor is very much a thing of the past, and if products can be made cheaper and faster somewhere else, they will be. Add to that Daniel Pink's book, *A Whole New Mind* (2005), and it is clear that to be productive on a worldwide scale, all students must be literate in new ways—such as the ability to see the big picture, to explain things in universal ways through means such as storytelling, and to empathize—even when they don't agree with the other person. The bar has been raised so high for education it is no wonder that droves of teachers leave the field each year in frustration. What can we do as educators?

The highest predictor of academic achievement is the proficiency of teachers in effective instructional practice. When we provide teachers with professional development on effective instruction (Effect Size = .98), teachers can override the impact of poverty (Effect Size = .76) (Wenglinsky, 2002). Effect size is a statistical measure of the difference in effect of a treatment, in this case a specific instructional practice, between a group that receives the treatment and a control group that does not, measured in standard deviation. This statistical measure can be converted to percentile point gains in achievement. (An Effect Size of .98 translates into 34 percentile points.)

Reading the study by Wenglinsky, we were moved not just intel-lectually, but heart and soul as well. The effect of poverty on student performance of .76 translates into an impact on achievement of 28 percentile points. Using the bell curve as a guide, let's say that the average child in poverty is at the 50th percentile. Then, if we had the power to remove the effects of poverty completely, we could move those children 28 percentile points in achievement to the 78th per-centile. Having taught in high poverty, high crime areas, we know the anguish of wishing you could somehow put your arms around these children and magically take away the effects of poverty. But as we have just seen, if educators received professional development on instructional practice and used it in the classroom, they would have enough impact to more than override the effects of poverty!

To make an even more significant difference in learning for chil-dren, teachers need to modify, or differentiate, these effective instruc-tional practices for context, content and product, and process in order to improve academic achievement *and* to close the gap in achievement for students from poverty, students of diverse cultures, and English-language learners. That is power that transcends education. It changes communities for the better. It affects economics, crime rates, literacy rates, education levels, and the housing market, and it strengthens democracy. A strong middle class is essential to a strong democracy. It is the middle class that has built the community, the schools, and the standards that affect us all. Can you think of a country in the world that is a democracy and does not have a middle class? There are none.

What We Can Do

This book empowers educators, because we not only provide the underpinnings and the rationale for looking at the effects of both culture and poverty; we also provide a research-based model for differentiation that is both practical and sound. In addition, for the first time, educators are provided with one model that accomplishes two purposes simultaneously: closing the gap for diverse learners *and* improving achievement. We do that by not only delivering the most effective teaching practices, but by modifying those practices to close the gap forever, as shown in Table 1-3 (Williams, 2003):

Table 1-3: Increasing Achievement—Closing Gaps

WE CAN DO BOTH	
Improving Achievement	**Closing the Achievement Gap**
• Curriculum, instruction, assessment	• Focus on the learner
• Title I, special education, gifted and talented, ELL programs	• Culture trumps poverty.
• After-school programs, tutoring	• Culturally responsive teaching
• Pacing guides, increased assessment, posting standards	• Honoring collectivist value systems
	• Building resilience
	• Differentiating context, content and product, process, and assessment for culture and poverty

Summary of Chapter One

In this chapter we looked at the relationship of poverty, culture, and race, how these factors intersect, and how they affect our children—especially diverse learners and children of poverty. We saw why deficit models don't work, and why we need a new differentiation model that accounts for culture *and* poverty. We introduced the four-step model and examined its three core areas: differentiating for context, content and product, and process.

The next chapter explains why we need a new differentiation model—one that addresses both the poverty and the racial achievement gap—and shows the research supporting this contention.

CHAPTER TWO

Differentiating for Economically and Culturally Diverse Learners

Teachers not armed with effective instruction cost students 20 percent per year in achievement.

—David Berliner

Differentiated instruction means instruction that has been modified to address the needs of the diverse learners in the classroom. If you had Googled *differentiated instruction* early in 2008, you would have gotten 397,000 results! Identifying the unique needs of children and adjusting the learning environment so that they can all achieve at high levels is a tremendous challenge for teachers. We cannot build resilience for children of poverty without addressing the impact of their culture on achievement. When teachers try to differentiate instruction for children of poverty, they cannot ignore their diverse cultures, ethnicity, and race—the sources from which students draw their background knowledge and experience.

Why Do We Need Another Differentiation Model?

As administrators and teachers, we used to say, "If you rank the schools in our district based on the socioeconomic status of the parents, you'll have the rank for student achievement as well." Like many, we used to believe that we could not do anything about the achievement of children of poverty, because we couldn't "fix" the poverty and therefore couldn't "fix" the children. This reflects an old paradigm of looking at certain children as "problems"—as having deficits they need to overcome in order to succeed. Nothing could be further from the truth.

As much as we care about our students, as teachers we cannot change the conditions under which they live. Those conditions may involve violence, homelessness, drugs, poverty, or any other number of things. Our students may speak languages we are unable to speak and come from cultures whose values we don't understand.

What we *can* do is teach so that our students learn and succeed in spite of the obstacles. We do this by becoming "turnaround teachers" who provide the conditions in school that ensure that all children achieve and succeed. It's not a quick fix. It requires a shift in beliefs, perspectives, and practices that begins with us.

Teachers everywhere have tried to differentiate instruction to meet the needs of the children in their classrooms. Their attempts are usually conditioned by their own perspectives, the "set of glasses" through which they look at human development and schooling. Most teachers in North America were raised in a middle-class environment and see through the lens of a Euro-American cultural value system. From that perspective, teachers have done an incredible job of empowering white, middle-class children to learn and succeed. Having the same culture and background as your students provides you with a context through which you communicate expectations, rules, beliefs, appropriate behaviors, and assumptions about human development and learning.

Children who don't have traditional Euro-American values have often had their educational needs met by someone other than the classroom teacher. These children were labeled special education kids, English-language learners, minority students, Title I kids, and gifted and talented. With the exception of the latter, the responsibility for differentiating instruction was often placed outside the classroom. The children placed in these programs were children of poverty (Title I), children of color (Title I and special education), and children new to this country (ELL).

What's Missing in Traditional Differentiation Models?

Whether we are attempting to improve achievement or close the gaps in achievement for diverse learners, our current models do not address the complexity of achievement gaps among racial and socio-economic groups. These models are missing the significant implications of culture and race and an integrated discussion of human development in varied cultural contexts. Williams (1996, 2003) notes that the focus of our interventions to improve academic achievement has been in the areas of curriculum, instruction, and assessment. But the focus of our interventions to close the achievement gap must be to attend to the culture of the learner and to build the supports necessary for learners to build resilience. As Williams writes: "All learners come to formal education with a range of prior knowledge, skills, beliefs, and concepts that significantly influence what they notice about the environment and how they organize and interpret it" (p. 5). This is the influence of culture—the means through which we learn and develop our own "set of glasses."

Children's culture defines what they will focus their attention on, how they interpret the world to give it meaning, what background knowledge they bring to learning, and how they will value that learning. As the National Task Force on Minority High Achievement and current assessment data from state tests show—with the exception of Asian Americans—minority students, even those who are not poor, tend to score lower on achievement tests than whites who are poor

(Manning & Kovach, 2003). Culture trumps poverty in its impact on achievement. To effectively deal with the issues of poverty, we must first deal with differences based on culture.

Education planning must also consider culturally differentiated patterns of academic preparedness. Traditionally, our models have described social-class influences—for example, poverty—as superseding ethnic-group effects. However, we now know that the achievement gap transcends social class (Daniels, 2002; Wang & Kovach, 1996; Wang & Reynolds, 1995). In North America, as in many other parts of the world, economic inequality is linked to both race and class.

A New Model Must Address Racial Achievement Gaps

In the 2007 STAR test results, according to California State superintendent of public instruction Jack O'Connell, we learned that *even when poverty is not a factor, the performance of black and Latino students is behind those of white children* (Mangaliman, 2007). California's STAR test results show that African Americans and Latinos who are not poor perform at lower levels in math than white students who are poor. O'Connell notes that "these are not just economic gaps, they are racial achievement gaps." In other words, simply trying to explain away the differences in test scores between Hispanics and whites or African Americans and whites as the fault of poverty no longer holds true. Past methods of remediation did not take into consideration the *culture* of the students; they did not account for the ways that so many of our schools are structured primarily to teach white students. They merely looked at the deficiencies in the test results. O'Connell stated, "Once again, these annual test scores shine a glaring light on the disparity in achievement between students who are African American or Hispanic and their white or Asian counterparts. We know all children can learn at the same high levels, so we must confront and change those things that are holding back groups of students" (Mangaliman, 2007). We must look at culture first to determine the very best methods for teaching these students and then provide the scaffolding and instruction to make them successful.

Linda Lane, deputy superintendent of the Pittsburgh Public Schools, has responded to a study led by Robert Strauss of Carnegie Mellon University on the achievement gap. Dr. Lane writes: "Poverty is a factor that affects achievement; however, *race is a larger factor* [italics added]" (Wereschagin, 2007, p. 1). The study noted that teachers who were successful in improving achievement were successful with both black and white children. That is, successful teachers address culture (closing the gaps) *and* achievement (instructional strategies).

A new model for differentiating instruction must view students from poverty as children with *differences* in culture and value systems, and in the ways they respond to unfavorable conditions in the dominant society—not as children with deficits that need to be "fixed."

Our research-based model for differentiating instruction in order to improve academic achievement *and* close the achievement gap will help teachers to deliver on this pedagogy.

Differentiating Instruction Using a Research-Based Model

Poverty has a negative impact on the academic achievement of our students. However, we also know that when we arm teachers with the knowledge and skills to successfully differentiate instruction for diverse learners, they can build in their students the resilience they need to override the impact of poverty. Modifying (or differentiating) instruction requires that we honor and respect the diverse cultures of students from poverty.

In 2004 and 2005, Learning Bridges (www.learningbridges.com) provided teachers in the highest poverty, lowest-performing schools in Maryland's Prince George's County with online professional development on the most effective, research-based instructional strategies aligned to their standards. This professional development was drawn from the Learning Bridges Aligned Instructional Database, which

A Pedagogy for Narrowing the Achievement Gap

Belinda Williams has identified the qualities of an educator who teaches to high academic standards:

- Has a clear sense of his or her own ethnic and cultural identity

- Communicates high expectations to all students, along with the belief that all students can succeed

- Is personally committed to achieving equity for all students and believes that he or she is capable of making a difference in students' learning

- Develops a personal bond with students and ceases seeing them as "the other"

- Provides an academically challenging curriculum that includes attention to the development of higher-level cognitive skills

- Focuses instruction, guiding students to create meaning about content in an interactive, collaborative learning environment

- Provides learning tasks that students see as meaningful

- Provides a curriculum that includes the contributions and perspectives of the different ethnocultural groups that make up the society around them

- Provides scaffolding that links the academically challenging and inclusive curriculum to cultural resources that students bring to school

- Explicitly teaches students the culture of the school *and* seeks to maintain students' sense of ethnocultural pride and identity

- Encourages parents and community members to become involved in students' education; parent and community members are given a significant voice in making important school decisions related to programs, such as resources and staffing

(Williams, 1996, p. 65)

aligns effective, research-based instructional strategies to the standards of every state in the United States. Embedded into that professional development were the modifications to close the gap in achievement for children of poverty, diverse cultures, and English-language learners (based on the Urban Learner Framework grounded in the research of Dr. Belinda Williams). The Maryland State Assessment (MSA), administered in the spring of 2005, showed that the highest-poverty, lowest-achieving schools in this region made significantly greater gains in achievement than the middle-class and affluent schools that did not participate. Most of the teachers chose Vocabulary Strategies as their first professional development class. There they also learned how to *modify* this powerful instructional strategy to address the learning needs of the diverse cultures in their classroom.

Table 2-1: Report on Prince George's County Public Schools—Region III

Grades	Fifteen High-Poverty Title I Schools Using the Learning Bridges System	Eight Nonpoverty, Non-Title I Schools Not Using the Learning Bridges System	Learning Advantage for Schools Using the LB System (Percentile Point Gain)	Learning Advantage for Schools Using the LB System (Percentage Advantage)
	Average Percentile Point Gains: Reading			
3	11.61	5.30	6.31	54%
4	11.91	9.33	2.58	22%
5	8.28	5.60	2.68	32%
6	6.04	5.16	0.88	15%
Improvement Range	4.1 to 19	(2.7) to 15.6		
	Average Percentile Point Gains: Mathematics			
3	10.03	7.68	2.35	23%
4	15.19	8.80	6.39	42%
5	12.48	11.01	1.47	12%
6			15.59	17%
Improvement Range	3.7 to 19.6	0.3 to 16.2		

The high-poverty, Title I schools using the Learning Bridges System *significantly* outperformed the improvements made by the nonpoverty and non–Title I schools in all grade levels and in both reading and mathematics.

The county has 135,000 students. Seventy-six percent of its student population is African American, 6% is Caucasian, 3% is Asian, 14% is Hispanic, and .5% Native American. Sixty-one percent of the children receive free or reduced-price lunches. Students come from

150 countries, speaking 149 languages (S. Gray, personal communication, January 15, 2005). Clearly, something happened in the classrooms! Using differentiated instruction, teachers made a significant difference in achievement for *all* of their students.

Summary of Chapter Two

Our four-step research-based model, which we explore in depth in the chapters to come, provides you with the knowledge and skills to translate differentiation into a workable model. That model addresses the reality that there is both an achievement gap and a racial gap in our schools. The four-step model discussed in the chapters to follow will show you how to accomplish the following:

- Build resilience in children of poverty and diverse cultures and recently emigrated children.

- Create institutional relevance for students of diverse cultures.

- Build on the personal and cultural assets that children bring to the classroom.

- Increase students' sense of efficacy and confidence both as individuals and learners.

- Build the background knowledge necessary to level the learning playing field.

- Activate prior knowledge and experiences to address new learning tasks, and to store and retrieve information through more than the semantic pathway to the brain.

- Recognize and respect relationships and social knowledge as critical to continued success.

- Create the brain-compatible conditions and high expectations that allow for the success of every child.

CHAPTER THREE

Building Teacher Background Knowledge

Being student-centered also means connecting learning to students' lives, using the student's own culture, strengths (intelligences), interests, goals, and dreams as the beginning point for learning.

—Bonnie Benard

To begin the shift in beliefs and instructional practices necessary to differentiate instruction, we need to examine our own background knowledge and experience. This is especially true for the majority of us who are part of the dominant culture. The first step in our model is to build teachers' background knowledge in order to expand the perspective provided by that culture. This is critical if we are to understand the needs of students from poverty and diverse cultures. As a way of examining our background knowledge as teachers, let's look first at two competing value systems.

Collectivist vs. Individualist Values

Well-documented studies have verified that two ways of thinking, or value systems—*individualist* and *collectivist*—have an impact on what teachers reward and punish in schools (Williams, 2003; Greenfield, 1994; Markus & Kitayama, 1991). Our value system—collectivist or individualist—is grounded in our culture and determines how we view achievement and value social knowledge. These factors affect our relationships with parents and the community, our approach to classroom management and organization, and our approach to curriculum, instruction, and assessment—the key processes in education that define our work.

In Table 3-1, we compare and contrast these two value systems so that we can identify the critical attributes of each.

Table 3-1: Collectivist vs. Individualist Value Systems

Collectivist	Individualist
Native American Indians, Native Hawaiians, Native Alaskans, Latin Americans, Africans, Asians, Arabs	Anglo-Saxon and Northern European Americans
Emphasizes interdependence	Encourages independence
Preserves relationships, which are hierarchically structured around family roles and multiple generations	Values individual achievement
Defines intelligence as knowing how to successfully play one's role in the family or community	Views intelligence as competitive and aggressive
Regards the purpose of physical objects, like toys, as mediating social relationships; they are valued because you can share them with someone else	Regards the purpose of physical objects, like toys, as developing skills in manipulating objects so children can become more competent and able to construct knowledge of the physical world
Communication includes proximal modes such as touching and holding.	Communication includes distal modes through linguistic means such as reading and writing.
Parents are more likely to promote their children's social intelligence and to emphasize interpersonal relationships, respect for elders and tradition, responsibility for others, and cooperation (relationship first; substance second).	Schools and parents define children's early cognitive development in terms of their knowledge of the physical world and linguistic communication skills (substance first, relationship second).

(Based on Small, 1998; Barakat, 1993; Greenfield, Brazelton, & Childs, 1989; Blake, 1993, 1994; Delgado-Gaitan, 1993; Kim & Choi, 1994; Suina & Smolkin, 1994; Hofstede, 1983; and Lebra, 1994)

Not Understanding These Value Systems Has Consequences

Schools in the United States emphasize individualism and independence as a goal of development. As teachers, we provide activities and opportunities for our students to interact that encourage them to make their own choices, take the initiative, and focus on logical rational cognitive skills over social development (Delgado-Gaitan, 1993, 1994). Unless teachers specifically provide children with an activity that requires collaboration (such as cooperative learning groups), when students help each other without our explicit direction, the school calls it cheating. *Cheating,* however, is a culturally relative term. Students from minority cultures grow up with very different values than their teachers with respect to helping each other and working together, and this creates a cross-cultural conflict for them. Other consequences of not being aware of these value systems include the following:

- The encouragement that children receive at school to be independent may undermine their sense of social affiliations and responsibility for others. What gets praised at school may get shamed at home, presenting a terrible conflict for the child.

- Schools may encourage a child to think independently and voice logical rational modes of arguing a point. However, this same behavior may get punished at home as disrespectful to elders.

- Schools may expect responses from the child on the substance of the content first, with observations about relationships second. But collectivist cultures emphasize relationships first and substance second. Children may preface an answer to a question like "Which food groups did you have at breakfast?" with a statement such as, "I help my grandma make breakfast for my brothers and sisters in the morning. . . ." When, unaware of the collectivist value orientation of the child that generated this response, a teacher rejects that answer or redirects the question to another student, that teacher is inadvertently devaluing the child's contribution and implicitly asserting the primacy of his or her own values.

Understanding Value Systems Has Great Benefits

On the other hand, understanding how these value systems affect our students has extremely beneficial effects. Teachers can use the information in a number of ways:

- To develop better relationships with parents—Parent-teacher relationships can become more personal, and teachers can take more advantage of opportunities to interact with parents before and after school. Seeing things from the parents' perspective creates better relationships with students and contributes to their success.

- To emphasize small-group conferences instead of individual conferences with parents—Collectivist moms and dads are often more comfortable talking in a group and focusing on a number of students rather than focusing exclusively on their own child (Quiroz, Greenfield, & Altchech, 1999). Teachers should consciously respect the concerns parents have about their children's social development, rather than discuss only their cognitive and academic development.

- To change your classroom management system and reorganize your classroom to allow students to help each other— Helping behavior is highly valued in many children's homes, and helping each other with classroom jobs such as putting away materials or storing equipment after use demonstrates an acceptance of that value.

- To provide opportunities for children to share materials—For example, Latino immigrant parents strongly value sharing over personal property (Raeff, Greenfield, & Quiroz, 2000). Have places in the classroom where "community property"— rulers, markers, protractors, and so on—is stored.

- To provide opportunities for students from collectivist cultures to integrate academic and personal information when responding to curriculum and instruction—As teachers pressured to cover the curriculum, we often get impatient with our students' telling of "stories." With the understanding of *why* students communicate in particular ways, we can respond more constructively, while honoring the culture of the home.

- To provide opportunities to participate collaboratively in literature circles and choral reading—Literature circles are somewhat like cooperative learning groups, where each student is responsible for part of the understanding of the work being discussed. In choral reading, students read aloud together in whole or small groups to practice the rhythm and sound of English without any one student being showcased.

- To *explicitly* teach both the value system of your classroom and that of the dominant culture—Make these rules, values, expectations, modes of communication, and ways of interacting apparent. Provide opportunities for these different value systems to influence and be incorporated into what is happening in your classroom. By giving them value, honor, and respect, you will implicitly value, honor, and respect your students as well.

Vocabulary and Crystallized Intelligence

We encourage all of our teachers to appropriately teach the vocabulary of the standards when they work with students. However, when we are seeking to improve academic achievement and close the gaps in achievement for children of poverty, students from diverse cultures, and English-language learners, teaching vocabulary takes on critical significance.

Let's quickly review what we know from research. We know that there is a statistically significant relationship between intelligence and academic achievement (Bloom, 1984b, 1984c; Dochy, Segers, & Buehl, 1999; Fraser, Walberg, Welch, & Hattie, 1987; Walberg, 1984). According to Ackerman (1996), we also know that intelligence is believed to be of two types: intelligence as knowledge (also known as *crystallized intelligence*) and intelligence as cognitive processes (also known as *fluid intelligence*). We make a distinction between the two because they should be taught differently, they are stored differently in the brain, and they are retrieved from memory differently.

Crystallized vs. Fluid Intelligence

Crystallized intelligence refers to what we have learned as facts, generalizations, and principles. It also includes skills that are specific to a domain, such as multiplication facts—for example, knowing that 4 x 4 equals 16 every time is a domain skill (Marzano, 2003). Most of what is taught in school outside of physical education and some technical courses falls into the realm of crystallized intelligence.

Fluid intelligence refers to the *processes* that are taught and used in school. Creating mindmaps and building models are process skills. Fluid intelligence requires crystallized intelligence. For example, to build a model of the brain, students need to know the parts of the brain, the size and shape of the brain, and so on.

A strong relationship exists between academic knowledge and crystallized intelligence (Rolfhus & Ackerman, 1999). Crystallized intelligence is also powerfully connected to background knowledge (also called prior knowledge) which all children bring to the learning experience. Marzano (2003) states that "crystallized intelligence is learned knowledge about the world; prior knowledge is learned knowledge about a specific domain" (p. 50). The most direct way of increasing students' prior knowledge is to provide them with very enriched experiences, such as trips to museums, field trips, and hands-on experiences with the world.

However, we know that many of our diverse learners, especially those from poverty, come to school with different experiences and with a different understanding of what "the world" is. They do not come with the enriched experiences of their middle-class counterparts, and they have half their vocabulary (Marzano, 2003; Nagy & Herman, 1984). For our children of poverty, children from diverse cultures, and English-language learners, direct vocabulary instruction—appropriately done—can build background knowledge and thus crystallized intelligence.

Vocabulary development is in fact a substitute way to measure crystallized intelligence, and correlates to academic achievement because of the nature of memory and the relationship between language and thought (Marzano, 2003; Chomsky, 1957, 1965).

This is very significant because some of our children do not have the vocabulary to describe even their own background knowledge and experience. As a result, they cannot bring that prior knowledge to learning a new task. Without it, the brain cannot make connections between new knowledge and known knowledge, nor can it find a pattern by which to "hook" new knowledge. This significantly impairs learning. Explicitly teaching vocabulary has many benefits, including the following:

- Increases language competence and ability to think in abstract ways

- Builds background knowledge, which is especially important when children have not had an enriched environment

- Increases your students' surface knowledge of new words that will form the basis for greater understanding of the content (standards) you are teaching

- Brings about dramatic gains in academic achievement, and if appropriately taught, can help to level the playing field and close the achievement gaps between groups of children—it increases *learning!*

High Expectations

McKinney, Flenner, Frazier, and Abrams (2006) suggest that urban children are likely to be victims of labels that communicate and foster low expectations. We have never met a teacher who *intended* to communicate low expectations for any child, but teachers do often have misconceptions about children of poverty and from cultures other than their own. As a result, they develop and adopt low expectations for them. Consistent exposure to these low expectations can lead to low self-confidence, lack of motivation, and poor achievement in students.

Most of us have heard about the significance of holding high expectations for children. (Again, we have never met a teacher who *intended* to communicate low expectations for any child.) When Brophy (1982) investigated urban teachers, he found that effective teachers believe that all children can learn *and* that they are capable of teaching the children successfully.

Teacher expectations are communicated and demonstrated in a variety of ways. For example, teachers tend to pay more attention, maintain more eye contact, and smile more at high achievers than they do at low achievers, and they ask low-level questions of students whom they perceive to be low achievers. Some teachers tend to give up on really challenging students, accept their failure, and even blame the students for it. Lavoie (1996) called this "blaming the victim," but in some cases, the failure may result from a teacher's incompetence or lack of understanding:

> Research clearly shows that teacher education students tend to view diversity of student backgrounds as a problem, rather than as a resource that enriches teaching and learning. Moreover, many of these future teachers have negative attitudes about racial, ethnic, and language groups other than their own. Such attitudes manifest as low expectations, which are then expressed in watered down and fragmented curriculum for children of poverty and diverse cultures. (Zeichner, 2003, p. 100)

We see the results of these low expectations playing out in the number of students of color and students from poverty placed in special education, expelled from school, and dropping out. We see the results, too, in the lack of diversity in many international baccalaureate classes, advanced placement, honor rolls, and classes for gifted students.

Successful teachers of students living in poverty and students of color are committed to assuring that all students achieve success; these teachers truly believe they can make a difference (Ladson-Billings, 1994).

What Must We Do?

- We must place fully qualified teachers who complete teacher education programs with students of color and students living in poverty.

- We must provide professional development in the elements of effective pedagogy that apply to a culturally diverse classroom. We *know* what has to happen. We need to find the will to assure that it does.

- We need to find teachers who truly believe that all children can learn (and that they are capable of teaching) and place those teachers with diverse learners.

- We need a "no-excuses" approach that lets students know we will never give up on them.

- We must find ways to both let our students know we see the potential they possess and to mirror it back to them. This is especially important to children "who have been labeled or oppressed, in understanding their personal power to reframe their life narratives from damaged victim or school failure to resilient survivor and successful learner" (Benard, 2003, p. 120).

Summary of Chapter Three

There are four important things for teachers to keep in mind to successfully approach the task of differentiating instruction. First, we need to remember that many cultural groups hold a collectivist value system that values sharing, collaboration, and a different view of learning than the Euro-American value system that is prevalent in schools today. Most American teachers identify with the individualistic value system and need to provide a way to teach the expectations of the dominant culture while finding ways to honor the value systems of our students' homes and communities—to show respect for their culture and, implicitly, for the students themselves.

Second, we need to remember that we can level the playing field with explicit instruction in vocabulary. In doing so, we build crystallized intelligence, one of the best indicators of academic knowledge. Crystallized intelligence is demonstrated by many school-related skills: the ability to recognize or recall facts, generalizations, and principles, along with the ability to learn and execute domain-specific skills and processes. We can close the vocabulary gap between our poor, minority children and our white, middle-class children and provide them with the background knowledge to learn new tasks.

Third, we need to create a culturally responsive classroom by finding ways to integrate the cultures of our students into the content we are teaching. Culture determines how children will view the world, where they will focus their attention, and how they value learning. Addressing the cultures in our classroom that may be different from our own will override the impact of poverty on academic achievement.

Last, we need to keep first and foremost in our minds the power of holding high expectations for *all* of our students. We need to remember to help them see the potential that they cannot see themselves. We cannot give up—ever!

CHAPTER FOUR

Planning to Differentiate

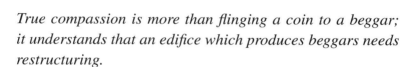

*True compassion is more than flinging a coin to a beggar;
it understands that an edifice which produces beggars needs
restructuring.*

—Dr. Martin Luther King, Jr.

You are now ready to plan to differentiate a lesson for your students. Our purpose here is not to describe how to plan a lesson for instruction, but on how to *modify* (or differentiate) a lesson plan to meet the needs of students from poverty and students of color. There are many ways in which teachers plan to differentiate for all students. What we want to focus on here are those specific planning considerations that are critical for students living in poverty and students of color. These are some of the considerations when planning to differentiate for diverse learners:

- Preteaching essential vocabulary

- Contextualizing the content and classroom for culture

- Modifying instructional strategies

- Determining grouping strategies

Let's look at these planning tools in the context of a hypothetical classroom.

Mrs. Jones's Third-Grade Language Arts Class

Most of the students in Mrs. Jones's third-grade classroom are eligible for free or reduced lunch, which indicates that they are living in poverty as defined by the U.S. government. The ethnic makeup of her students is 60% African American, 30% Hispanic, 9% white, and 1% Native American.

The language arts lessons she has planned for her students meet the following standard:

Uses reading skills and strategies to understand and interpret a variety of literary texts

Here are the third-grade learning expectations for the standard:

- Knows the defining characteristics of a variety of literary forms and genres (for example, fairy tales, folk tales, fiction, nonfiction, myths, poems, fables, fantasies, historical fiction, biographies, autobiographies, chapter books)

- Understands the basic concept of plot (for example, main problem, conflict, resolution, cause-and-effect)

- Makes connections and comparisons between characters or simple events in a literary work and people or events in his or her own life

Mrs. Jones has identified three learning objectives for her students based on these standards:

1. Know the defining characteristics of various literary genres.

2. Be able to connect events and people from a story to their own lives.

3. Understand the basic concept of plot.

As Mrs. Jones plans this lesson, she wants to meet the unique needs of the diverse learners in her classroom. In order to do that, she must incorporate in her planning how she will differentiate for the cultures represented in her classroom, and how she will provide the means for all of her students to learn these objectives.

Preteaching Vocabulary

The first task for Mrs. Jones is to identify the essential vocabulary that her students will need to accomplish her learning objectives. As an initial source for the essential vocabulary, she explores the language of the standard she has selected. She determines that the following terms need to be taught:

- Autobiography
- Biography
- Characteristic
- Fable
- Fairy tale
- Fantasy
- Fiction

- Folklore
- Genre
- Historical fiction
- Myth
- Nonfiction
- Poem
- Realistic fiction

Mrs. Jones knows that preteaching these terms will build background knowledge for her students, especially those living in poverty who may not have had access to books of this nature. She also knows that preteaching these terms will provide an opportunity for her students from diverse cultures to activate any prior knowledge and experiences they have had with these words.

Her strategy for preteaching the vocabulary for diverse learners will be to use a nonlinguistic organizer called an attribute wheel. This organizer will allow her students to create pictures that represent the critical attributes that define each of the genres of literature. An example of an attribute wheel is shown in Figure 4-1.

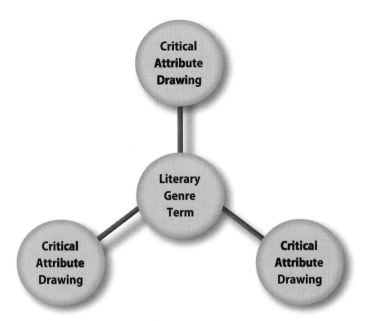

Figure 4-1: An attribute wheel for literary genres

Mrs. Jones plans to have her students work in pairs to complete the attribute wheels after she has taught each vocabulary term, so that they have an opportunity to help one another. She prepares examples of attribute wheels with vocabulary terms in them as examples of quality work, so that her students can see visually what her expectations are for this task.

We believe the most powerful process for teaching vocabulary is Marzano's six-step process:

1. Students receive a brief, informal explanation, description, or demonstration of the term.

2. Students receive an imagery-based representation of the new term.

3. Students describe or explain the term in their own words.

4. Students create their own imagery-based representations for the term.

5. Students elaborate on the term by making connections with other words.

6. Over time, teachers ask students to add new information to their understanding of the terms and to delete or alter erroneous information. (Marzano, 2003, p. 62)

Contextualizing Content and Classroom for Culture

Mrs. Jones has predominantly African American and Hispanic children in her third-grade class. She plans to greet each student at the door and personally welcome them each morning. As she plans lessons to teach the various literary genres, she makes sure to select examples from cultures of the ethnic groups in her classroom. She also selects stories that reflect a range of reading abilities and interests, including these:

- *Amazing Grace,* by Mary Hoffman. Grace proves she can be the best Peter Pan in spite of classmates telling her she can't because she's female and black (Dial, 1991).

- *Chicken Sunday,* by Patricia Polacco. Winston, Stewart, and their "sister friend" want to buy a special gift for Miss Eula for Easter, but are falsely accused of throwing eggs at the local shopkeeper. This is a story of intergenerational and interracial friendship and creativity (Philomel, 1992).

- *Mufaro's Beautiful Daughters: An African Tale,* by John Steptoe. Mufaro's two beautiful daughters go before the king, who is choosing a wife (Morrow, 1987).

- *Drylongso,* by Virginia Hamilton. This is a mythical story about a mysterious young boy named Drylongso, who appears at Lindy's Midwestern farm just before a big dust storm hits (Harcourt Brace Jovanovich, 1992).

- *Just Like Martin,* by Ossie Davis. In 1963 Alabama, Stone meets Dr. Martin Luther King, Jr., and wants to be a preacher, but his father sees nonviolence as cowardly and refuses to embrace it (Simon & Schuster, 1992).

- *Justin and the Best Biscuits in the World,* by Mildred Pitts Walter. Ten-year-old Justin jumps at the chance to visit his cowboy grandfather, at whose place he traces his black cowboy ancestors and learns that cooking is not just "women's work" (Lothrop, 1986).

- *Amelia's Road,* by Linda Jacobs Altman. Amelia, the daughter of migrant farm workers, learns to cope with moving from harvest to harvest while dreaming of a stable home (Lee & Low Books, 1993).

- *Magic Dogs of the Volcanoes / Los Perros Mágicos de Los Volcanes* (bilingual), by Manlio Argueta. English translation by Stacey Ross. This is a colorfully illustrated folk tale of the magic dogs that live in the volcanoes of El Salvador and protect the villagers from harm (Children's Book Press, 1990).

- *Cesar Chavez: Labor Leader,* by Maria E. Cedeno. This traces the accomplishments of the labor leader who fought to improve the lives of Mexican American farm workers in California (Millbrook Press, 1993).

In preparing her classroom, Mrs. Jones puts up posters of different authors drawn from the various genres. She makes sure to include African American and Hispanic authors among the pictures. She creates a bulletin board that is divided into the various literary genres, and in each section posts book covers of stories from that genre, making sure to reflect the cultures in her classroom.

Mrs. Jones also places students' desks in groups of four. They form a semicircle around the area where she will teach. She plans to also use this space for student presentations and student-led activities.

Modifying Instructional Strategies

Mrs. Jones has chosen a number of strategies to teach the objectives she has identified. In her planning, she will address the modifications for these strategies to meet the needs of the diverse students in her classroom.

She has chosen the following instructional strategies:

- Compare and contrast
- Call and response
- Critical thinking skills
- Double-entry journal
- Grouping students

Compare and Contrast

She will use the compare and contrast strategy so her students will be able to identify similarities and differences among the various genres of literature following the teaching of the critical attributes of each. She will modify this strategy by combining it with a grouping strategy to meet collectivist needs. She will also modify this strategy by utilizing a visual graphic representation for students to demonstrate their understanding. Mrs. Jones plans to let children choose between a Venn diagram and a T-chart as their graphic representation. She will encourage students to think aloud as they work in groups.

Call and Response

Mrs. Jones plans to use an African American form of call and response involving a *griot* to introduce and close each day with an affirmation about the specific tasks to be accomplished during the unit. The griot in African society is skilled in storytelling and serves as a poet, historian, teacher, singer, and entertainer. Mrs. Jones prepares the first affirmation ahead of time and will teach the concept and process of the griot to her class on the first day of the unit. We will discuss call and response strategy in more detail in the next chapter.

Critical Thinking Skills

As part of her planning process, Mrs. Jones prepares a graphic organizer for her students to record their classification of 12 stories according to their genre. Students will work collaboratively to classify the stories based on the attribute wheels they have created. Each group will present their graphic representation to the entire class with their verbal justification for their classifications by genre.

As part of her planning process, Mrs. Jones also prepares a graphic representation for her students to analyze a story of their choosing and to represent the basic elements of plot in small groups. She prepares two different graphic organizers from which the groups can choose.

Plot and Conflict Analysis

Student's Name: _____ Date: _____

Title: _____ Author: _____

1. Did you feel like you were part of the story?
   ❏ Yes   ❏ No   Explain your answer.

2. Were you able to guess what was going to happen at the end?
   ❏ Yes   ❏ No   Explain your answer.

3. What do you think was the best part of the story?

Conflict List (check one or more)

   ❏ Character vs. Nature

   ❏ Character vs. Self

   ❏ Character vs. Society

   ❏ Character vs. Character

1. What was the main problem in the story?

2. What was the character's goal?

3. How was the problem solved? (resolution/solution)

Story Map
Setting (where and when):
Major characters:
Minor characters:
Plot:
Event 1:
Event 2:
Event 3:
Outcome:
From *Plot and Conflict Analysis and Story Map.* Copyright Mariely Sanchez, 2008. Used with permission.

Mrs. Jones plans to provide her students with the opportunity to analyze several stories from the same genre and decide as a small group which of them best meets the critical attributes of that genre. They will then present their findings as a group to the whole class, complete with their rationale for their decisions.

As a culminating activity, Mrs. Jones plans to have her students write or create a skit, a rap, or a song that contains the critical attributes of one of the genres, using one of the classroom stories they've read as a model. Students will work in groups to select their genre and story, identify the elements of the genre, and then choose what form to use, containing all the critical elements, to model the genre.

Double-Entry Journal

Each student in Mrs. Jones's classroom has a journal. In this unit, Mrs. Jones plans to ask the children to divide two pages of their journal in half by drawing a line down the middle of each page. This creates two columns on each page. At the top of the left column, she asks them to write "Stories by Others," and at the top of the right column she asks them to write "Stories by Me." In the left column, they write or draw events (or identify characters) from the stories they are reading that remind them of something that has happened to them. In the right column, they write or draw the event (or the character) in their life about which the story reminded them. The double-entry journal provides a powerful way to reflect on stories and how they relate to their world. They are personal journals to be shared with the teacher only. Sharing of journals between students is done only at the initiation of a student.

So far, Mrs. Jones has done the following:

- Selected effective instructional strategies to use to teach her students

- Planned to modify them for her diverse learners by providing many opportunities to work in groups, honoring the collectivist value system of most of her students

- Planned individual, metacognitive activities with the use of personal journals and opportunities for verbalization of thinking, which allows the brain to dually encode the thinking process

- Planned to allow her students choices in how they will demonstrate their learning

- Planned for the culturally responsive call and response strategy as a chance to lead, chorally respond, provide for movement, and enhance self-concept as a learner

- Planned for examples of quality work and the use of models from which they can connect known to new knowledge

- Planned to provide access to content examples drawn from students' cultures

Grouping Students

Most of Mrs. Jones's students come from cultures that value working together, and in which the group's goals supersede individual goals. She has planned activities for her students that honor the cultural values represented in their homes and families. There are many ways to allow students to work together and help each other, including pairs, cooperative groups, and any number of small group situations. Mrs. Jones plans to have her students share materials, leadership, and the presentation of learning. Students will never feel singled out in her classroom.

Planning Differentiation for a Secondary-School Classroom

The examples that we have provided for Mrs. Jones's classroom show how planning can be conducted in an elementary setting. What about secondary classrooms which range from 45 minutes to 120 minutes depending on the type of schedule used in the school? Here is an example of planning for a secondary classroom. The basic planning pieces are the same.

Preteaching Vocabulary

Always teach vocabulary first. Whether students are learning about atoms or genres, unless they understand the language of the subject, they will not be able to fully understand the lesson. We recommend that vocabulary be taught in a series of seven words or less. This follows how the brain learns best. If the lesson requires 20 new vocabulary words, teach them in chunks of seven. We also recommend that secondary students keep a vocabulary notebook using a setup similar to the one in Table 4-1.

Table 4-1: Notebook Setup for Vocabulary Words

Vocabulary word or words	My understanding of the words	Formal definition	My definition	Graphic for remembering
1.				
2.				

In this organizer, we give students the words up front, prior to the lessons. Next, they are asked what they already know about them. We are tapping into prior knowledge and making certain our students do not have misconceptions about the terms.

In the next step, the teacher gives a brief and concise formal definition of the word(s) to the students. The teacher may want to give examples and nonexamples (what the word is and what it is not). Then the teacher teaches the words in the context of the lessons.

After teaching the lesson, the teacher asks the students to put the definitions into their own words. Learning needs to be personally relevant to the brain for long-term memory to occur (Tileston, 2004b).

It is important to provide our students from poverty with a visual to help them retrieve the meaning from long-term memory. Most of the cultures of the diverse classroom are visual or visual-kinesthetic. By asking students to draw something in order to help them remember the term, we are providing one more structure to help them. For ELL students, for example, the picture gives a context to the learning, so that on those days when they need to remember, they will likely remember the picture first and then the word.

Providing Personal Objectives

Always provide the objectives of the lesson and ask secondary students to provide in writing their objectives for their own learning. Not only do we want our secondary students to be cognizant of the objectives required by the state and school, we also want to give the learning personal meaning. We want our students to learn to plan themselves and to be able to identify whether they are meeting their personal goals, and if not, why. Throughout the lesson the teacher will refer back to the goals, both instructional and personal, and ask the students to evaluate their own progress.

Grouping Students

Throughout the lesson, provide opportunities for students to discuss the learning and to share ideas. Students might create visual maps together in groups of two or three. Again, there are many ways to allow students to work together, help each other, and share materials, presentations, and group leadership.

Summary of Chapter Four

In this chapter, we looked at the second stage of our model—planning to differentiate. Teachers everywhere plan and incorporate differentiation into every lesson to meet the individual needs of their students. But most of those plans for differentiation were created for the dominant culture. Our focus here has been on planning to meet the needs of our students living in poverty and students of color. We have illustrated four major areas:

1. Preteaching essential vocabulary

2. Contextualizing the content and classroom for culture

3. Modifying instructional strategies

4. Determining grouping strategies

These four considerations specifically meet the needs of the diverse learners in our classroom.

In the next three chapters we turn to the core area of our differentiation model: how to differentiate context, content and product, and process.

CHAPTER FIVE

Differentiating Context

> *We are beginning to realize that a lot of these things which are supposed to be universal are actually culturally specific and without pathological consequences if they deviate from contemporary American norms.*

> —Robert A. LeVine

In this chapter, we explore strategies for creating culturally responsive classrooms for students of color and students living in poverty. Culturally responsive classrooms have two critical attributes: 1) the inclusion of students' languages, cultures, and daily experiences into the academic and social context of school; and 2) explicit teaching of the dominant culture's expectations, so that all children can fully participate (Zeichner, 2003). In some urban schools, alternative certification is being offered to permit community members to become teachers. To be culturally responsive, we have to build bridges between the culture of the school and the cultures of the home and community.

We also explore the characteristics of effective teachers in multicultural classrooms and look at research-based instructional strategies they can use that have a powerful impact on diverse learners. In addition, we provide examples for African American and Hispanic students, the two major minority groups in the United States.

What Is a Culturally Responsive Teacher?

Children dealing with the effects of poverty, violence, family dysfunction, and adverse neighborhood conditions have a far greater likelihood of entering school without the skills, competencies, and emotional intelligence they need to be successful in the classroom. This is especially true for poor students in inner-city neighborhoods, many of whom are from racial and ethnic minorities. These children pose a huge challenge for teachers who must provide equal access to educational opportunities. Those of us who want to have an impact must take specific actions to reflect the cultural values and diversity of our students (Banks, 2001). The leading researcher in urban teacher education, Martin Haberman (2005), identified the characteristics of teachers who are effective with diverse learners in urban school settings:

- Effective urban teachers are persistent and constantly pursue strategies and activities so that all children can be successful.

- They take responsibility for their students' learning, including the learning of students at risk.

- They relate theory to practice and translate innovative ideas into classroom practice.

- They develop rapport and cultivate personal relationships with their students.

- They are capable of adjusting to and coping with the demands of bureaucracy.

- They take responsibility for their own mistakes.

- They possess emotional and physical stamina, which allows them to endure the challenges and crises of urban settings.

- They have organizational and managerial skills.

- They understand that teacher success is achieved by effort and hard work, not just ability.

- They are committed to meeting the individual differences of students, with no excuses.

- They engage in active teaching, not just direct instruction.

- They create a classroom environment in which students feel needed and wanted.

- They find approaches that will assist students in mastering the materials.

- They have a belief system that is promising and provides hope, and they offer gentle teaching in a sometimes violent society.

- They lead students toward both social and academic success.

Creating a Culturally Responsive Classroom

Creating a culturally responsive classroom requires that we help students find a way to work collaboratively toward the goal of using, developing, and constructing knowledge. There are five major principles of a culturally responsive classroom (Shade, Kelly, & Oberg, 1997):

1. The learning environment is inviting.

2. The community leader sends personally inviting messages.

3. Teachers manage an inviting classroom with firm, consistent, and loving control.

4. An inviting learning community communicates that the students can accomplish the task being asked of them.

5. An inviting learning community stresses collectivity rather than individualism.

The Learning Environment Is Inviting

You regard students as contributing members and establish a physical and psychological environment that allows them to feel at home.

Students believe they know how to function within this environment and that it will satisfy their basic needs. The classroom is stimulating and arranged for easy movement. The colors, lighting, sounds, and physical arrangement of the space attract children to the learning process. The placement of the desks enhances relationships instead of blocking them—relationships between you and your students as well as among the students themselves.

The Community Leader Sends Inviting Messages

You send personally inviting messages, both verbally and nonverbally, indicating that you are caring, accessible, and dedicated, and that you hold high expectations for all your students. Students sense that they are special and important, and this is evidenced in their facial expressions, dress, and persona. By communicating patience, understanding, enthusiasm, and flexibility, you inspire in your students a sense of self-worth and pride in achievement.

The Teacher Applies Firm, Consistent, and Loving Control

Everyone wants to have a sense of belonging, especially in places where they spend a great deal of time. In the middle-class classroom, teachers struggle with how to effectively create an inviting environment while maintaining order as well. According to Shade, Kelly, and Oberg, "The differential use of discipline creates the most cultural conflict as social control mechanisms used by teachers of culturally different students are significantly different from those used by the students' parents" (1997, p. 51). You manage your classroom in a manner that eliminates the conflict between home and school. And you are not ruled by the fear—based on a lack of knowledge about the culture of your students—that if you give up an inch of control, you will lose control and chaos will reign. You address student misbehavior privately and never single out or reprimand students in front of the group. Aware of the community and homes from which your students come, you observe how their parents and caregivers manage their relationships with them. Especially with African American and Latino children, you separate your response to misbehavior from your response to the child, knowing that if students perceive a withdrawal of caring, they feel rejected and regard such a response as inordinately cruel.

Students Believe They Can Accomplish the Tasks Asked of Them

Communicating to students that they can accomplish the tasks before them creates a positive academic self-concept. Students from poverty and students from diverse cultures often come to school with self-concepts in all areas but academic self-concept (Shade, Kelly, & Oberg, 1997). You understand that many of them are wounded by the rumor of inferiority and that achievement in school for some represents the loss of their ethnic identity and is perceived as "acting white." You do not ask students to choose between Anglo-American culture and their own. By mirroring your students' assets back to them, you let them know you are aware they possess potential they are unaware of themselves. You always communicate that you believe your students can achieve, you expect them to achieve, and you will not give up on them—no matter what!

The Community Stresses Collectivity Rather Than Individualism

You are aware that in many cultures the family or peer group is often more important than the individual. In his work on motivation, Triandis (1990) observed that this difference in values between individualism and collectivism is probably the most important cultural difference that can be identified. It determines whether children will pursue and value their own individual goals over those of their tribe, family, and work groups, or whether they will place collective goals ahead of their own. Seventy percent of the world's population live in cultures that value reciprocity, obligation, duty, tradition, dependence, harmony, and an emphasis on family integrity and interdependence (Triandis, 1990). By being inclusive, by respecting collective action rather than overvaluing individualism and competitive interaction, you eliminate some of the conflict your students feel.

Instructional Strategies for Culturally Responsive Classrooms

As you deliver instruction to your diverse learners, think about strategies that best meet their unique needs. The following teaching practices are known to encourage culturally diverse students, including those from poverty:

- Cooperative learning
- Graphic representations
- Wait time
- Affirmations

- Group investigation
- Call and response strategy
- Visual imagery
- The KIVA Process

Some of these strategies apply to all diverse learners; others are more appropriate for specific cultural groups. To help you make choices for your students, we will give brief descriptions of each.

Cooperative Learning

Cooperative learning involves student participation in small groups to maximize learning for all. It enables learners to achieve a specific goal, to communicate with other students and help each other with learning tasks (so important for collectivist cultures), and to demonstrate individual and group accountability. It also develops social skills as students process their achievements within the group and monitor and evaluate the results.

A critical component of cooperative learning is providing a way to check that *each* student is learning. Without it, this strategy will have significantly less impact on academic achievement (Darling, 1999). Explain, model, and guide students in how to think critically and work collaboratively. Compose your groups, furnish resources, and structure tasks so that students must depend on one another for personal and group success. Provide a resource-rich, positive, and safe environment for students to achieve their individual and group goals. Encourage the positive and productive interaction of all team members, and provide time for reflection. Cooperative learning can affect achievement by as much as 28 percentile points (Darling,

1999), in addition to meeting the unique needs of diverse learners. It can also be delivered with other instructional strategies, such as concept mapping, to add to its effect on learning.

Group Investigation

This strategy, also called *inquiry,* presents students with an area of investigation, helps them to identify a conceptual or methodological problem, and invites them to design ways to overcome it. It does this by requiring them to process information by observing, collecting, and organizing data; identifying and controlling variables; and formulating and testing hypotheses and explanations. It is a natural strategy for culturally responsive, student-centered classrooms, in which students bring diverse cultural perspectives to any issue. Once they have drawn inferences about the data and the results, students present that information to the group. The steps of the group investigation-inquiry process are as follows:

1. Students encounter a puzzling situation (planned or unplanned).

2. The teacher and students explore reactions to the situation.

3. The students formulate a study task and organize to study the situation (problem definition, role, assignments, and so on).

4. The students engage in both independent and group study.

5. The teacher and students analyze progress and process.

6. The teacher and students refine the original puzzling situation and recycle through steps.

This strategy can involve having students interview people in the community, storytelling, students writing from their own experiences, inviting community members in to share information, or using technology for research, art, music, and so on. It has applications for all cultural groups and can result in as much as a 37 percentile point increase in learning (Darling, 1999).

Graphic Representations

Graphic representations come in many formats for achieving a variety of purposes. They are wonderful, because they can be used either by individual students or groups to record their thinking. Table 5-1 shows correlations between specific types of graphic representations, brain function, grade level, cognitive process, and memory path.

Table 5-1: Graphic Representations Correlated to Brain Processing, Level of Schooling, Instructional Process, and Memory Path

Name	Brain	Level	Process	Memory Lane
KNLH	Relevance Patterning	Elementary Secondary	Reflect Connect Evaluate	Semantic Episodic
Fat Skinny	Relevance Patterning	Secondary Adult	Compare Analyze Hypothesize	Semantic Emotional
T-Chart	Relevance Patterning	Elementary	Analyze Compare Associate	Semantic
Mapping	Emotion Relevance Patterning	Secondary	Brainstorm Analyze Compare Connect	Semantic Episodic
Analogy/Simile	Emotion Relevance Patterning	Elementary Secondary	Synthesize Brainstorm Associate Connect Reflect Visualize	Semantic Emotional Episodic
PMI	Emotion Relevance	Elementary Secondary Adult	Connect Reflect Analyze Associate Evaluate	Emotional Semantic

From *Graphic Representations* by Shelley Roy. Copyright 2000 by Learning Bridges. Reprinted with permission.

Concept mapping, a graphic representation showing relationships among ideas using words or pictures, is a powerful tool for diverse learners. A concept map consists of a circle in the center of the page with spokes. At the end of each spoke is another circle.

When we want students to show the critical attributes of a concept, we put the concept name (or a picture that represents it) in the center circle. Each circle at the end of a spoke contains a defining attribute of that concept—either in words or pictures. Concept mapping is a great tool for embedding information into long-term memory and can produce as much as a 49 percentile point gain in achievement with our diverse learners (Darling, 1999).

The KNLH Chart has four columns in it with the letters *K, N, L,* and *H* at the top of each column (see Figure 6-2 on page 93). Either individually or in groups, students write in what they already **K**now under the K, what they **N**eed to learn under the N, what they **L**earned under the L, and **H**ow they learned it under the H. The KNLH chart allows students to bring in experiences and skills rooted in their own cultures.

Call and Response

As we have seen earlier, this is an excellent strategy to use, especially with many of our African American students, and is based in a cultural pattern that renews energy through its expression (Shade, Kelly, & Oberg, 1997):

1. A vision or message activates the emotional and spiritual power within each of us.

2. This creative power expresses itself through music and rhythm—in song, dance, or drums.

3. Some form of participation reinforces the power of the vision or message that in turn empowers each individual and collective group. This form of participation connects the mind and body in total engagement.

The "caller" sends a message to the group ("responders") who immediately affirm the individual power and unique style of the caller. This strategy provides an opportunity for everyone to participate. It reinforces the memory of the message because of the repetition and choral response. It is multisensory, and all children can have a turn leading the group. The griot activity is an example of call and response.

Wait Time

Wait time is a strategy that most of us know about but often forget to use. When you ask a question of the group, count to five slowly before either calling on one individual or signaling the group to respond chorally. This allows for individual differences in the brain's response time. This strategy is appropriate for all diverse learners. (You can read more about wait time on page 121.) Providing thinking time for your students can create as much as a 40 percentile point gain in achievement (Darling 1999). That's worth waiting for!

Visual Imagery

This strategy has power to help immigrant students develop English skills and provides a natural connection between previous learning experiences and new learning. Students recall an image from their past and use their imagination to expand it. A new, enriched image is then formed, which the individual students draw, adding more detail to the drawing as they learn more, and labeling it with both their native language and English words. This takes an idea from a figural basis (an image in the mind's eye), to a symbolic basis (a drawing representing some meaning), to a semantic basis (words representing the drawing). For example, in our mindmap drawing, students might use words in their native language as well as pictures to represent the features of animal migration. The teacher would then lead them to add the words in English. Using the words in their native language with the drawing as a bridge to the English words will help these students store the information in a context. Since English-language learners often do not have the vocabulary skills to recall information appropriately, providing the context of the drawings helps them to experience easier recall.

Affirmations

This strategy is often used in both African American and Native American cultures. One affirms oneself relative to the collective community or the universe. It allows students to relieve inner conflict and focus their actions during the day, and it integrates personal and collective values. Teachers can choose affirmations that reinforce the concepts students are learning, that acknowledge that children come to school with cultural experiences that must be honored, and that reinforce them as academically successful students. Ask children to stand in a circle facing each other. The leader recites the affirmation (this can be the teacher or a student) and then asks everyone to be silent for a minute. The followers then echo the affirmation. This is repeated three times. Then the leader asks everyone to be silent for a minute again to think about how this affirmation will help them today. Students then leave the circle. Use this at the beginning or end of each day, or both.

The KIVA Process

The KIVA process, developed by Lila N. Carol (1993), had its beginning in Pueblo Native American tradition. Shade, Kelly, and Oberg (1997) adapted it for culturally responsive classrooms. It can be used to identify a problem, analyze it, and resolve it with a consensus process for students. KIVA honors every voice in the room, so it may take several days to complete. Change your classroom space so that tables and chairs are arranged in a circle. Place other chairs in concentric rings around the tables. The teacher or leader then stands or sits in the center and asks essential questions related to the issue. The participants sitting at the tables have 10 minutes to respond to the questions. They then stand up and move to the outer ring. The ring next to the tables and chairs sits down, and now it is their turn to respond to the essential questions about an issue. This continues until every person has had a chance to share. Recorders write down both the questions and the responses. At the end of the rounds, the participants prioritize the responses to indicate either the most important problem or best solution from the discussion. When KIVA reconvenes, the facilitator synthesizes the viewpoints represented and identifies where the significant differences are. Students then identify the themes that have evolved. There may need to be further clarification. The leader tries to articulate the consensus of the group.

KIVA might be used for such issues as the following: Should students be required to wear uniforms? Why or why not? Should students attend school year round? Why or why not?

The Culturally Responsive Classroom

Let's see how these instructional strategies can be put to work in two situations. We'll look first at African American learning styles and then at a fictional classroom of predominately African American students. Then we will look at the learning styles of our Mexican American students and at a fictional classroom made up of primarily Mexican American children.

The Culturally Responsive African American Classroom

Because of the loss of self and identity through slavery and segregation, all too many African Americans are preoccupied with simply surviving in a hostile world. Certain cultural traits have evolved to protect the psyche and help students adapt to a hostile world (Pasteur & Toldson, 1982; Gay, 2000, 2002). As a result, many African American children have ways of perceiving and thinking that are different from white children.

Perceptual Style

We have had an explosion of knowledge about the brain, including how the brain prefers to learn. We call these modalities of learning. Ninety-eight percent of all new learning comes through the senses, and based on our past experience with learning, we are more likely to learn if information is presented in the modality most comfortable to us. Researchers such as Tileston (2004b), Jensen (2004), and Sousa (2005) tell us that visual learners prefer to take in information through images; they prefer to learn by watching and observing. Auditory learners prefer the verbal presentation of ideas, like storytelling. Tactile learners like to hold, touch, or manipulate materials.

Although many students from the African American community have a multimodal perceptual style, the majority of information in our society, particularly the information in schools (90% of it!), is transmitted through the visual channel. Villegas (1991), Shade (1993), and Gay (2000, 2002) have noted that these children prefer oral presentations, social interactions, and tactile information. When acquiring information, they prefer nontextual visual media, such as pictures, photographs, symbols, and multisensory approaches (including movement, images, verbal communication, and sound). Many African American children need to be physically and socially active in school. Male African American students are five times more likely than male Anglo-Europeans to initiate conversation with others, to act out to get attention, or to move around in the classroom (Morgan, 1990; Weinstein, Curran, & Tomlinson-Clarke, 2004). In our own observations of classrooms, we've seen that many African American students express their personalities, movement, and body style through their walk, hair, and dress, and during games and dance through a love for rhythm. Understanding the ways culture affects how students interpret their world helps us, as teachers, to identify ways to modify instruction for them. When we stop perceiving our students' culture as an obstacle and accept it as part of the learning process, it becomes a valuable addition to the learning process.

Attentional Style

Our cultural community socializes us to pay attention to certain kinds of cues—emotional cues about how other people feel toward us, spatial cues to help us orient ourselves in our own environment, and object cues that provide information about things in the physical environment. Many of the African American students in our classrooms pay more attention to the people in their environment than the objects or things. Because of this, they are better able to distinguish emotions, recognize faces, and pick up nuances in social situations than many European Americans (Ruble & Nakamura, 1972; Gay, 2000, 2002).

Along with where they focus their attention, these students have a response style that leans more toward extroversion than introversion (Myers, 1980; Gay, 2000, 2002). This means they get their energy from and direct their actions toward other people as a means of self-expression. In classrooms, we can best focus their attention if they are in groups and if we present information at a constantly changing pace. These students tend to prefer processing information aloud with others. Sometimes, we call it "thinking aloud." Teachers need to understand that this is not a strategy for avoiding learning or of socializing during class time, but another way of processing information.

Conceptual Style

The amount of information bombarding our brain requires that we sort it, categorize it, or lump it together in some way to process it. Many African American children use different categories than European Americans to do this. A number of authors, including Rychlak (1975), Gay (2000, 2002), and Villegas (1991), suggest that our African American students prefer materials and contexts with affective or socioemotional meaning to more impersonal material. This means that the learning tasks we put before them should have some relationship to their experience of reality—in other words, it must be relevant to them. These children are more likely to learn content that is related to their culture and their community.

Thinking Style

We find more children in the African American community who synthesize information easily than children who work in a sequential, detail-oriented process. From the work of researchers such as Shade, Kelly, and Oberg (1997), we know that "research on cognitive processing styles indicates that African Americans are more likely to consider information in a holistic, relational, and field-dependent manner than are Anglo-Europeans" (p. 72).

Putting It Together

The description of a culturally responsive classroom that follows is an adaptation of one provided in *Creating Culturally Responsive Classrooms* (1997), by Shade, Kelly, & Oberg.

The classroom is airy and inviting, with lots of red, black, and green. The room sets the tone for high expectations, pride, a sense of belonging, and academic excellence. The teacher greets each student at the door, perhaps using an African greeting of "*Jambo*." Students sit at tables of four, arranged in a semicircle to face the teacher as they wait for the affirmation period. One student is the griot for the day.

GRIOT: Greetings, brothers and sisters.

CLASS: Greetings, Griot. *(Group claps three times.)*

GRIOT: Today's affirmation is, "I have solved problems like this before."

Individual students interpret what the affirmation means to them and how it relates to the work they must do for the day. They also relate how the affirmation will help them to be successful in their respective tasks.

GRIOT: The Griot is finished.

CLASS: Thank you, Griot. *(Group claps three times.)*

The teacher divides the class into three instructional areas. In the smaller one, three students work to identify possible African American personalities that they will portray in the school's African Notables performance next month. Their table is soon covered with a variety of academic resources on science, math, philosophy, history, economics, and geography. When teaching math or science, the teacher weaves examples from African American culture into the lessons wherever possible. When teaching how to write a persuasive essay, she chooses content that speaks to her students' lives.

The students, engaged in discussions, sit close together and communicate animatedly, using body language and gesturing. Bookcases filled with multicultural literature line one wall. Photos and prints of authors, many of them African American, hang above the bookcases. A couch sits off to the side under a window with pots of flowers. Two students sit at opposite ends of the couch. The one with headphones is listening to Beethoven and silently reading *Why We Can't Wait,* by Martin Luther King, Jr. The other is taking notes on *The Autobiography of Malcolm X.* They are preparing for a debate on the philosophies of these two great leaders of the Civil Rights Movement.

The second space in the classroom has computer stations where groups of students work on a variety of projects—for example, comparing the cultural geography of Africa and North America, predicting and graphing the seasonal migration of birds from information found on the Internet, or writing to a textbook editor in response to something they have just read. This area also contains CDs and videos. Two students are classifying American music from the late 1800s to the present. Their hands drum the rhythms on the table.

The third space is larger, with tables arranged so that students can sit in groups of four to facilitate cooperative learning. Resources in this space include a chalkboard and science materials. The wall contains the student classroom management wheel for cooperative groups and individual responsibilities. It also has the state's content standards and performance expectations for achievement. The tables are used to create a theater area in which the rest of the students are practicing their individual parts for the Notables performance. One student practices his part, and other students use a rubric to provide him with feedback on his performance to help improve it.

The day ends the way it began—with the griot. They hold hands and close their eyes, and the griot repeats the affirmation for the day. The griot asks them to reflect and visualize their day and their tasks. They are silent for 2 minutes. The day closes by repeating "*Harambe*" seven times with hands in the air to signify unity, purpose, and their sense of responsibility to each other.

Teachers who want their classrooms to reflect cultural diversity of their students should ask themselves these questions:

- How is this classroom different from most classrooms?

- What social patterns are evident?

- How should I differentiate instruction for my students? Do they have an opportunity to recognize and affirm their identification with people of African descent?

- Do they have an opportunity for mutual responsibility?

- Is the curriculum personally meaningful? Can they recognize and maintain the cultural values of their community?

- Is there an opportunity for critical thinking and inquiry?

The Culturally Responsive Mexican American Classroom

The U.S. Census Bureau reports that the Mexican American population grew from 22.4% in 1990 to 35.3% in 2000 and projects that Mexican Americans will constitute 47.8% of the population by 2010 (U.S. Census Bureau, 2006). In contrast to African Americans, however, there are few studies of the cognitive style of Mexican Americans. Because we also know that there are Hispanic and Latino children in our schools from countries other than Mexico, we have to weigh what little information we do have carefully.

Perceptual Style

Ramirez and Castenada (1974), in a view supported by Gay (2000, 2002), believe that many Mexican American children are field-dependent—that is, they perceive globally and experience new information holistically. They see and appreciate relationships and learn best when material has social content. They attend best to materials relevant to their own experience but require an organizational framework to help them. And because of their strong family ties and respect for and obedience to elders, they tend to internalize criticism from their teachers and elders. Interestingly, as these children become more acculturated in the mainstream, there is more evidence of field independence, which is more typical of European Americans.

Conceptual Style

Language is an important issue for many Latino families. They enjoy verbal play and the use of jokes and humor, similar to the verbal play used by many African Americans. These provide a release of tension and are often used to defuse conflict, since arguing is usually considered rude and disrespectful. Diplomacy and tact are valued communication skills (Shade, Kelly, & Oberg, 1997; Gay, 2002).

Social Interaction Style

Mexican American children tend to work well together, participating in cooperative or collective efforts. It is important in this community to develop strong interpersonal relations—the strong extended family is representative of this value. Experiencing life to the fullest is a good descriptor of the predominant response style of Mexican Americans, who seek rewards and self-satisfaction when they are personally involved with people, ideas, and events (Ramirez & Castenada, 1974; Gay, 2000, 2002).

In our classrooms, we need to remember that many of our Mexican American children identify closely with their community, family, and ethnic group and are very sensitive to the feelings of others. Role definitions, especially those for males and females, must be respected. In this culture, achievement and success are generally regarded as highly dependent on the cooperative efforts of individuals rather than competitive individualism (Ramirez & Castenada, 1974; Gay, 2000, 2002; Weinstein, Curran, & Tomlinson-Clarke, 2004).

Linguistic Style

Villegas (1991), Kagan and Zahn (1975), and Shade, Kelly, and Oberg (1997) have all suggested that we cannot understand the culture of Mexican Americans without understanding the significance of their language. For our Hispanic children, the Spanish language represents their heritage and culture; in many cases it is the primary means by which they communicate their feelings. Yet even though Spanish is one of the world's greatest languages and ranks second among languages most spoken in America, it has low prestige in most of the United States.

The Mexican American community is faced with a dilemma. On the one hand, they seek assimilation and acculturation. On the other, the community is constantly reinfused with people who bring with them the culture and language of Mexico; many individuals, in fact, travel back and forth between the two countries, maintaining their previous frames of reference. Without a clear break in ties with the country of origin, its language and values remain strong.

As teachers, we need to help our students maintain their identity with their cultural and ethnic background *and* develop an identity as Americans. These are important goals for all of our children. In the United States, the debate has not concluded as to whether we can best accomplish this through English immersion, bilingual education, or special classes for English-language learners.

Putting It Together

Students in this culturally responsive classroom are excited as one of them puts his hands into the opening of a large, green, cardboard box, called the Mystery Box. The opening is covered with a piece of material, so no one can see what's inside. Other students in pairs and with varying levels of English proficiency try to describe and identify the objects in the four boxes that have been placed on a round table in the science area of the classroom. Aquariums are located on top of bookcases, beneath a window. Brightly colored fish fascinate the students. Also on the bookcases are terrariums designed by the children to show different habitats, as part of their study of the effect of the environment on animals. The room has pictures of plants and animals found in the children's native countries, labeled by the students in both English and Spanish.

Other bookcases and storage cabinets are arranged to create small group areas. Around the corner from the science area is a fine arts area. An ELL teacher is working with a group of 10 children who are learning a song to reinforce their spelling words for the week. They have created their own musical instruments. The teacher is using mnemonic strategies to teach the children vowels. She teaches them a rhythm pattern, and they chant the letters to the beat of their instruments. She also uses the piano to help students learn vowels by listening to the notes and holding the long and short vowel sounds. Music and sound help embed the learning. A video camera in the corner of the fine arts area is available for taping individual and group performances used to monitor progress on language acquisition. Storytelling, rhymes, limericks, and jokes help students learn new sounds in a fun way. This center also provides a natural forum to share cultural celebrations through music, song, dance, and drama. It's stocked with community materials like crayons, colored chalk, clay, paint, construction paper, poster board, and other art supplies to enhance multisensory learning.

The next area is a writing laboratory. One wall is covered with student-designed comic strips, a blend of reality and fantasy, in both Spanish and English. The artwork is very detailed, with vivid colors. The comic strips show a common theme of family life, with self-portraits of the students and their extended families.

Beneath the comic strip display are shelves with student portfolios and journals. A small group is busy writing and editing a class newspaper article about a student survey they have conducted to compare and contrast favorite American and Mexican foods. (Pizza is still the favorite!) Another wall of the writing lab has a poster listing the steps necessary to revise and edit written work. Students use rubrics to self-evaluate their work and give and receive feedback from fellow students.

The last area of the classroom is a combined book and game laboratory in which a visitor from the Chicano Community Center is working with students using games like Sea of Vowels and Where in the World Is Consonant City? Card and board games draw students to this center for ongoing reinforcement in syllabification, phonics, thinking strategies, and comprehension skills. Students hold tournaments in the classroom, and winners get to select a favorite book to read and then take home to read to their families. The students take turns reading aloud. They have an organizer to create a story map for the plot, characters, and setting. The organizer helps to integrate both global and analytic processes, because some languages are more pictorial and others are more semantic.

In this classroom, students have an opportunity to recognize and affirm their identification with people of Mexican descent. They have an opportunity to experience a sense of mutual responsibility and a chance to engage with a personally meaningful curriculum. In school they can recognize and maintain the cultural values of their families and their community, while engaging in critical thinking and inquiry.

A Checklist for Culturally Responsive Environments

To create culturally responsive environments that are inviting to your students, in which they feel affirmed and have a sense of belonging, consider doing the following (Shade, Kelly, & Oberg, 1997):

1. Use color and designs—for example, ethnic cloths, prints, artwork, and so on.

2. Provide a variety of kinds of multimedia, with students able to listen to music through headsets.

3. Plan opportunities for creative expression, such as dance, visual arts, choral reading, music, and graphic arts.

4. Build on previous experiences from your students' culture using hands-on learning, and create space for activities and a climate in which they can take risks and feel safe enough to have more questions than answers.

5. Arrange tables and desks to facilitate cooperative learning.

6. Involve students in the room arrangement and change it often.

7. Position your desk to send a message of collaboration rather than authority.

8. Plan long- and short-term interest centers.

Summary of Chapter Five

In this chapter, we examined the characteristics of teachers who are successful in improving achievement and closing the achievement gaps for children of poverty and diverse cultures. We explored the five principles that need to be followed if we want to create a culturally responsive classroom: 1) a learning environment is inviting; 2) the teacher communicates inviting messages to the students in various ways; 3) the teacher manages the classroom with firm but loving control; 4) the students have the conviction that they can accomplish what is asked of them; and 5) the learning community stresses collectivity rather than individualism.

We glimpsed the cultural patterns of the two dominant minority groups in the United States, and what a culturally responsive classroom that honored their cultures might look like. And we looked at culturally responsive instructional strategies that meet the needs of our diverse learners. Together, these techniques and strategies enable teachers to differentiate through *context*—creating the kind of classroom that can meet the needs of our students.

In the next chapter, we will explore how we can differentiate instruction according to the *content* to be learned and the *products* that children create to demonstrate their understanding.

CHAPTER SIX

Differentiating Content and Product

Eighty percent of students who are recommended for special education placement are below grade level in reading.

Sixty-three percent of African American fourth grade students are below grade level in reading.

Seventy-four million Americans read below the eighth grade level.

Eighty-five percent of juveniles coming before the courts are functionally illiterate.

Seventy percent of prison inmates are illiterate.

—Jawanza Kunjufu

In this chapter we will discuss the differentiation of content and product—two major pieces of the teaching and learning process. Our emphasis here is on content, because without quality and meaningful content, product does not matter. Content should lead to innovative and quality products that reflect understanding of the subject matter.

Differentiating Content

You may not think that you have much say about the content you teach in your classroom. After all, we live in an age of scrutiny in which we must teach to standards and prove that they have been taught. In this chapter, we will examine several ways that you can differentiate content to meet the unique needs of your students, yet still meet the expectations of standards. We will view content differentiation by looking at three key aspects of content in the classroom: relevance, rigor, and relationships, with our primary focus on relevance.

Relevance

Teaching for relevance is critical if we are to tap into students' motivation to learn. Research has verified its importance. The brain decides quickly whether the information it is receiving is worthy of its time and, if not, discards it. In fact, we discard about 99% of all incoming information (Jensen, 2004). No wonder kids don't remember all the information we give them. Making content relevant has the potential to increase student performance by as much as 40 percentile points (Darling, 1999)!

Detecting Bias

One reason that content seems irrelevant to many diverse learners is its cultural bias. That is why one of the first suggestions we make to educators is to examine the culture of their schools. Often they will tell us they are sure that they have rid the school and staff of any bias; but on closer inspection, there are sometimes surprises. Many formerly white middle-class neighborhoods have become communities with diverse cultures and larger numbers of children of poverty. Yet, we often find classroom materials still geared toward the interests of a Euro-American student population. Here are some things to look for when eliminating bias in teaching materials and content:

- Do any of the content materials reflect cultures other than Euro-American culture?

- Do the library and classrooms offer content of interest to students of various ethnicities?

- Does the content always portray people of non-Euro-American cultures in positions of authority and leadership?

- Are computers and books available for students to use?

- Do the visual materials (pictures, graphics, and so on) reflect the ethnicity of the classroom?

- As material is presented, does the teacher include the contributions of minorities and women where appropriate?

- Are the learning styles of the cultures within the school taken into consideration when materials are created for the classroom?

Providing a Personal Application

We are constantly bombarded by information—often too much at one time. Our brains, wired to survive, take about 15 seconds to decide whether to process and store information or to toss it out. That is why learning has to make sense and have a personal meaning for the learner to pay attention (Jensen, 1997). No wonder there is a saying in the sales world, "What's in it for me?" When deciding whether we will pay attention, we look for personal meaning—for ways that something helps us to fulfill an individual goal.

If you are reading this book, it is probably because you are hoping that it will provide an answer or help you to meet a goal personally or professionally.

We talk a great deal in the field of education about motivation and the lack thereof. But if learning has no personal relevance to our students, or they cannot see any practical application beyond the classroom, they will memorize information for a test and then promptly forget it. If students from poverty have low motivation to go to school in the first place, they will probably just tune out the teaching altogether. After all, they think, "How has school helped our parents, our grandparents, or our friends?" In *Hip Hop Street Curriculum,* Kunjufu (2005a) tells how he makes the importance of learning real to African American students. He explains that out of one million boys and girls who want to go into the NBA, only 35 will actually make it, and only seven of those will become starters. Even if they do, a player has a shelf life of about 4 years. He goes on to say that 86% of NBA players are African American, and only 2% of doctors are African American. What does this have to do with relevance? If we are to lift students out of poverty, we must give them enough information to help them make critical choices and to rethink old ideas about how to achieve. That may include teaching about careers, how the economy works, and how poverty is perpetuated.

Not everything you teach in school can have personal meaning to everyone, but to the extent possible, show students the real-world connection to learning. How does *Hamlet* relate to the issues a student may deal with in the neighborhood, on the streets, or in the classroom? The themes of corruption, lust for power, loyalty, and betrayal in Shakespeare's play are still with us—they repeat themselves over and over through time. The more our students learn about such human frailties, the more likely they are to be successful in dealing with life outside the classroom.

Using All the Senses

Figure 6-1 is a graphic example of how we take in information from the senses and store and retrieve it in memory.

Ninety-eight percent of all new information comes to us through taste, smell, touch, hearing, and sight (Jensen, 1997). Take a few minutes to reflect on how you use these senses to teach. We love the PBS video *Good Morning, Mrs. Toliver,* in which a real-life teacher of mathematics in Harlem inspires her students to use all their senses to help them learn and remember. For one lesson she dresses as a pizza chef and brings in pizza dough, which she twirls as she sings Italian music; she cuts the pizza into slices to teach fractions. Her students are on the edge of their seats. Whether they know it or not, every time they eat or even smell pizza or hear Italian music, they will probably think of fractions.

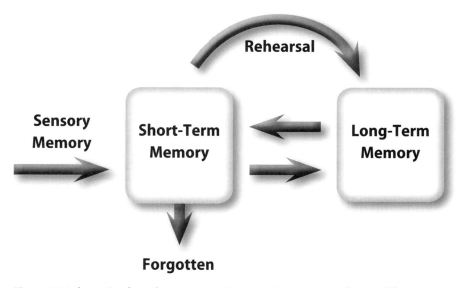

Figure 6-1: Information from the senses goes into short-term memory first, and if necessary is moved into and retrieved from long-term memory.

You may be thinking, "I am not going to sing in my classroom!" It's true that not everyone has the talents of Mrs. Toliver, but you can make your room a place in which sounds, visuals, smells, touch, and taste—where appropriate—help to teach the lesson. Ask yourself the following:

How does my room look? Stand at the door of your classroom looking in as if you were a student. What do you see that would make you want to learn? How have you used visuals? Even if you have wonderful objects in your room relating to learning, do they speak to your student population? Do the pictures, posters, and other information on the walls, the ceiling, the whiteboard, and the windows reflect the ethnicities and worlds from which your students come? For English-language learners especially, visuals are critical to learning. In fact, according to Jensen (2004), between 85% and 90% of the students in any given classroom are visual learners. If your primary method of teaching is to lecture, to what percent of the class are you teaching?

How does my room sound? Do I demand quiet at all times? Are the students expected to sit quietly and work or to listen to you and take notes? Do you provide ample opportunities for them to talk, question, and discuss? We are born into this world with about 50% of our "wiring" in place; the other 50% comes from the environment after birth (Jensen, 2004). If a child is constantly bombarded by a multimedia world day and night, his or her brain is set up to take in information in that fashion. Reinforcing that pattern is the greater amount of everyday noise that many children of poverty live with. As a result, they approach new information visually and kinesthetically. Then they get to school after 5 years of this and are expected to suddenly turn into a "brain" that learns by sitting and listening quietly all day. In fact, if we look at the general student population, only about 14% or less of those in a given classroom learn by hearing. And that figure is going down rapidly because of technology (Jensen, 1997). These students prefer to *see* information first, then hear it. When they can't, they become fidgety and drive us crazy.

How does my room smell? Using scents to create pleasant aromas in the classroom can make a difference in how it feels to spend time there. Next time you are at the mall, notice the stores as you walk by; the merchants pay a great deal of attention to the way the store smells in order to draw you in and make you comfortable.

Do I allow movement? Have I tried to accommodate the kinesthetic learning styles of my students? Many urban learners are accustomed to learning things by doing. They need manipulatives, tactile materials, and the opportunity to try things out. If a student who comes from a culture where movement is important is forced to sit quietly all day, discipline problems are inevitable. An effective teacher will provide opportunities for movement in the classroom and will make use of tactile materials and manipulatives for projects, products, and other hands-on activities (Carroll, 2001).

What kinds of books are available in my classroom? What kinds of materials do you use? Do they reflect the students that you teach?

Are there a variety of interests evident in the materials? If 63% of African American fourth graders are reading below grade level (Kunjufu, 2002) and you are a fourth-grade teacher with African American students, you may need to examine your reading materials to see if they reflect topics that appeal to African American children. In his book, *Black Students, Middle Class Teachers,* Kunjufu (2002) says that sometimes, after his workshops, teachers will tell him that they are color blind—that they treat all children the same. Kunjufu says that he asks to visit those classrooms, because bulletin boards, lesson plans, and library collections do not lie. Are the classrooms of your school a "cultural mosaic" of students?

In my classroom, do the students have opportunities to learn for themselves, to explore, to fail, and then try another approach? How much of the classroom time is direct teaching or lecture? How much of the time are the students engaged? Truly engaged?

Do I provide a wide variety of content—not just from the textbook? Use all of the senses. If you are talking about a particular time in history, bring in the sounds of that period with music or other media. Use all kinds of music, including rap, in the classroom to help students learn and remember. Kunjufu advocates teaching that matches the way children actually learn:

> If our children can memorize words from a rap CD, they can also remember the Constitution, the names of all 50 states, algebraic equations, and more. Children learn in different ways. The million-dollar question is: Can we put aside our ditto sheets, textbooks, and lectures and come up with new methods that incorporate the many different ways children learn? (2005, p. 83)

Teaching for relevancy provides authentic, real-life applications for new information during the teaching and learning process. These connections assist learners in activating their prior knowledge and storing new learning into long-term memory. They facilitate students' ability to generalize the learning to new situations. Students should also learn to use advanced organizers in order to illustrate connections between new and known knowledge and to reflect on the new learning through speaking and writing (Spangler, 2001).

Teaching for relevancy also encases "contextual learning" experiences for students. Research shows that urban learners especially benefit from this approach. Contextual learning, drawing on its roots in constructivist learning theory as well as theories of cognition and learning, has the following characteristics (Carroll, R., 2001):

- Emphasizes problem-solving

- Recognizes that teaching and learning occur in multiple contexts

- Assists students in learning how to monitor their learning so that they can become self-regulated learners

- Anchors teaching in the diverse life contexts of students

- Encourages students to learn from each other

- Employs authentic assessment

What Is the Role of the Teacher?

Teachers who are actively employing teaching for relevancy as a strategy in their classrooms provide applications from the real world—the world outside school—as a context for students to learn new material. They prompt students to activate prior knowledge of topics using advanced organizers or other means to connect new knowledge to known. Authentic assessments—for example, products, projects, observations—are a means for students to demonstrate their learning, provide clearer understanding of student comprehension, and require specific feedback. Included in the lesson plan is self-reflection on the new material, which aids students in long-term retention (Spangler, 2001). For example, in the study of geometry, we tend to spend a lot of time worrying about formulas for calculating volume and surface area. In order to embed these formulas into real concepts in a real-life context, we can devise a project that will not only teach but assess as well.

The Sticky Finger Fudge Example

Break students into "design teams" and ask them to design and produce a package in which to market "Sticky Finger Fudge" (Spangler, 2001). The package must hold between 100 and 125 cubic inches of fudge. Give the design teams parameters for the production of the packages, such as the cost of the cardboard, the cost of each color of ink, and so on. Each team must design and build an appropriate box and then make an oral presentation of the design to the board of directors of the Sticky Finger Fudge Company. Each presentation must be accompanied by a flat pattern of the box, including dimensions and computations, a colored rendition of the design, a written explanation of the process, and results. As presentations are made, students take turns acting as members of the board of directors. They review designs and check the computations of other students to determine if the demands of the board have been met.

At the end of the project, the board of directors, which by now includes all students, must determine which of the teams should be awarded the contract for the fudge boxes. Each student must make a written recommendation, detailing the reasons for his or her selection. When the topic is approached in this manner, students make fewer conceptual errors. One common mistake students make is forgetting to include the areas of one or more sides of the rectangular solid, but when they actually have to build the box, they don't forget. Reviewing designs as a "board member" provides students with the opportunity to practice computation skills and reinforces the use of the formulas. The ideas of design, advertising, marketing, and commerce become familiar, and students see them as valid occupations for real people. The culmination of the project is the recommendation for awarding the contract. Students must think about the various elements of the assignment, and reflect on the success of each team's presentation. In addition to meeting math objectives, students also polish skills in public speaking and written communication.

Relevance and the Learning Process

Our brains are structured to both process and store information according to what kind it is and how we will use it. What did you eat for dinner last night? What are the names of the seven dwarves? Both questions can be answered with lists, but the types of information are dramatically different. Dinner is something that happens in the context of our normal lives—we absorb this information casually and don't have to work to memorize it. The seven dwarves, on the other hand, are a novelty whose names we may or may not have committed to memory through repeated practice. These two examples reflect what research tells us are the two categories of long-term memory—taxon and locale (Spangler, 2001).

Taxon Memory

Taxon memory is structured to remember things in lists, such as states and their capitals, the rules of Monopoly, the causes of the Civil War, the seven warning signs of cancer, or the digits of your social security number. Such memories move into long-term storage only after repeated rehearsal, and the motivation to remember is extrinsic—for example, grades, money, or rewards. Because they are related to specific circumstances and are very resistant to change, it is difficult to apply or transfer taxon memories to similar situations. In addition, these memories may be disjointed and have no attached meaning. (How many youngsters carefully recite the version of the alphabet that includes the letter "ellimenoh" instead of *l, m, n,* and *o?*) The taxon memory structure is designed to recall memories on demand, but the demand must be specific. ("Spell *Massachusetts.*")

Locale Memory

The other component of long-term memory is locale memory, which consists of a series of "snapshots" taken in various situations as you progress through life. They include the music that played in the background, people who were present, conversations, the colors of the walls, and lots of other seemingly unconnected details. If the smell of spaghetti sauce makes you sad, it may be because your sense of smell is tapping into locale memory, to pull out the last visit you had from your grandma. The snapshot preserves the entire situation, linking the disparate parts in long-term memory. Locale memory is always contextual and survival-oriented. Everyone has this ability and uses it without conscious thought. It is intrinsic and motivated by your innate curiosity, your need to make sense of what is going on around you. Table 6-1 shows an example of the difference between taxon and locale memory.

As we plan for teaching, we need to capitalize on the structure and organization of the organ that will store all of the wonderful knowledge we want to pass on. Understanding how memories are enhanced by sensory connections helps us recognize why teaching for relevancy requires that material be contextual: It puts the learning in line to be caught by one of those clever snapshots that locale memory is taking to put into its "scrapbook." When planning for contextualized lessons, be inclusive of your urban learners, children of poverty, and culturally diverse students. Their contexts may not be the same as those of your Anglo-Saxon students.

Table 6-1: Taxon and Locale Memory

Classroom One: Taxon Memory	Classroom Two: Locale Memory
Students use flash cards to drill one another. Timed tests are given weekly, and children earn stickers for excellent performance.	Students play a game of "Kingdoms," where dimensions of their rectangular territories are earned through various classroom activities. Students keep track of their earned territories.
Extrinsic motivation (rewards, stickers)	Intrinsic motivation (playing)
Isolation of content	Contextualization of content
Nonsensory	Sensory
Difficult to transfer knowledge	Simple to transfer knowledge

Used with permission of Learning Bridges.

Taxon memory is an important part of how we think and learn, but memorizing facts and locking them away to use later is not enough. *How* the memorization takes place is critical. Like leftover veggies, this information will spoil if it is not combined with locale memory and made into some sort of memory soup! Children *should* memorize some material, but when you ask them to do so, it is necessary to recontextualize the material into useable information that is available for transfer and can be applied in a variety of situations (Spangler, 2001).

Multiple Intelligences and Relevance

Educators have become more and more concerned with the science and art of teaching. Previously, we expected students to learn regardless of the method we used and thought that those who could or would not learn were simply determined to be dull. We measured their abilities as mathematical or verbal, period. Many of our children of poverty, however, value other types of intelligence—often more than math and verbal skills. We need to begin looking at the gifts our students bring—at the kinds of intelligences they possess. One way that we can do this is through Howard Gardner's *Intelligence Reframed* (1999).

Gardner acknowledges the traditional intellectual strengths—the ability to process written, oral, or numerical material, but he adds others. As Carroll reports (2001), Gardner argues that there is both a biological and cultural basis for these multiple intelligences and believes that culture plays a large role in their development. Different societies value different types of intelligence: The cultural value placed upon the ability to perform a certain task provides the motivation for someone to become proficient in that area. Often, this capacity is misrepresented as talent, but Gardner specifically refers to it as a "way of knowing"—a way that individuals encounter and understand information. Each of us has a unique combination of these intelligences, some stronger than others. To date, Gardner (1999) has identified eight ways of knowing:

1. **Logical-mathematical**—Acuity with numbers and a capacity to reason effectively

2. **Verbal-linguistic**—The capacity to use words orally and in writing

3. **Visual/spatial**—The ability to perceive the visual/spatial world accurately and act on these perceptions

4. **Musical**—The capacity to perceive, discriminate, transform, and express musical forms

5. **Bodily-kinesthetic**—The ability to use one's whole body to express ideas and feelings

6. **Interpersonal-social**—The ability to perceive and discern between the different intentions, motivations, and feelings of other people (includes a sensitivity to nonverbal messages)

7. **Intrapersonal**—A capacity for both self-awareness and self-knowledge as well as an ability to adapt oneself through self-evaluation

8. **Naturalist**—The ability to make distinctions and form classes among plants, animals, and other parts of the natural environment and man-made objects

Learning styles and modality preferences tend to vary from one ethnic group to another. For example, African American and Hispanic students tend to be more hands-on, kinesthetic learners. This reflects the cultures from which they come, which rely on learning by doing. In contrast, there are cultures, particularly some Asian cultures, where students learn by listening (verbal linguistic) (Carroll, 2001).

When planning lessons, teachers need to consider multiple representations of material in order to capitalize on students' innate ways of understanding. Ideas embedded in real-world contexts are rich with opportunities to use alternative approaches to learning.

The following activities can connect the study of the Holocaust to what students perceive as their real world (Spangler, 2001), approaching the topic from a variety of angles and engaging multiple intelligences:

- Read *Anne Frank: The Diary of a Young Girl* (verbal/linguistic; interpersonal).

- Invite a speaker who survived the concentration camps and afterward produce a skit using the presentation as a base (verbal/linguistic; interpersonal, bodily/kinesthetic; visual/spatial).

- Use a variety of graphic representations to demonstrate the numerical value of six million, the number of Jews who died in the camps (mathematical/logical; visual/spatial, naturalistic).

- Compare events of World War II in Europe to events in the modern world, and write diaries from the perspectives of people involved in other world crises (interpersonal; intrapersonal).

- Hold a debate comparing fascism to democratic, parliamentary, and communist forms of government (mathematical/logical; interpersonal).

- Perform songs written as propaganda by both the Allied and Axis powers. Compare the positions echoed in the songs to the historical record (musical; logical/mathematical).

Gifted practitioners of the teaching arts have learned to use all eight ways of knowing to help *all* students gain meaningful knowledge. Not only does this approach make the material more "digestible" for many students, it makes it more interesting for everyone else in the classroom, too.

Teaching for relevancy is a constructivist practice that allows students to build their own meaning from instruction and encourages independent thought.

Learning Must Make Sense

Anytime we put out new information, there's a moment of chaos in the brain while it searches for what it already knows that can be attached to the new learning. We said earlier that 98% of all new learning comes from the senses. The other 2% comes from prior knowledge that is attached to the new learning. Our students are more likely to "get it" from the beginning if we can find ways to either tap into prior learning or—if there are no prior experiences or learning—create them. A lesson plan we like that illustrates this principle well is *Explorers Through Time,* from the McREL database (www.mcrel.org). In this unit of study, the teacher wants her students to not only understand some key pieces of history, but also to see that there are patterns to exploring anything new and that we all have to problem-solve to be successful.

She begins the unit by asking students to talk about something that they wanted very much and leads them, using a graphic organizer, through the constraints and restrictions they faced as they tried to reach their goal. She will later use this same kind of graphic to also help students look at the constraints that the explorers had to overcome.

A demonstration unit that we use in our training shows how to help to make connections between new learning and what the student already knows. This unit, on the subject of immigration, uses a KNLH chart, as shown in Figure 6-2.

What We Know	What We Need to Find Out	What We Learned	How We Can Learn More
Categories of information we expect to use:			
1. Politics			
2. Medical issues			
3.			
4.			
5.			
6.			
7.			

Figure 6-2: A sample KNLH chart

In the chart, the *K* stands for "know." Find out up front what your students think they know about immigration. Sometimes they will say before a new unit, "We already know all about that; we had it last year." This is a good opportunity to find out. Usually, you will find out that they do not know as much as they think they do; on the other hand, if they do already know quite a bit, adjust the pace of the lessons and go into in-depth learning. The *K* in our example means ask the students what they already know about immigration. Ask them to work in study groups of three and to answer this question by listing at least five things that they know.

At the bottom of the graphic organizer are categories 1, 2, 3, and so on. Ask the students to look back at the information that they listed and to put a 1 by anything that is related to politics. Next, ask them to put a 2 by anything related to medical issues. You will be discussing seven categories in the lessons of the unit. By giving students the categories at the beginning and applying them to what they already know, you are preparing their brains to make connections.

The *N* stands for "need to know." (There was a time when we would say, "What do you *want* to know in this unit?" We do not want to give students the chance to respond with "Nothing," so we now say "need to know.") This list comprises your students' personal goals. Children of poverty often do not make goals or plan for the future, and especially if they are surrounded by violence, they may believe that they have only today to think about. This exercise begins to teach them to set personal goals. After the unit is complete, revisit what they said they already knew and what they needed to know to determine if they have met their goals. Ask them to make a list of what they have learned and how they learned it. It is also important for children of poverty to understand how they are learning so that they see that it is their own efforts, their own processing that have led to the learning. We are trying to change their perception of locus of control, so that they come to realize it is not bad luck or good luck but their own efforts that lead to the learning.

Predicament at Pokeweed

One example comes from a wonderful book called *Snowed In at Pokeweed Public School,* by John Bianchi (1991). In this book, a group of children get snowed in and have to spend the night at school with their teacher and principal. In advance of the learning, ask students what they would do if they were snowed in overnight at school. Provide pictures of children playing, crying, doing art work, singing, reading, and so on, and ask them to circle the pictures that represent what they would do. Later, compare and contrast what the students in our school said they would do with the choices that were made in the story.

A Moral Dilemma From O. Henry

A middle school example is based on a well-known short story by O. Henry, "After Twenty Years." In this story, two young men make a pact on graduation night that in 20 years they will come back to the same spot at the same time and talk about what has happened in their lives. This is a great story for all students but especially for children of poverty, because it deals with issues that many of them face in their own lives. Prior to reading it, ask them first if they would turn in someone they knew who was wanted by law enforcement if they knew that person's whereabouts. Then ask them how it would affect their decision if they worked in law enforcement. Figure 6-3 is an example of a graphic organizer you can use to ask students to make their decisions. It is a continuum in which students place the number of the question along the continuum line, based on what they would do. In this case it obviously does not work for the student to reveal the person's whereabouts. Later, compare and contrast their decisions with the actual decisions made by the characters in the book.

After Twenty Years by O. Henry

Figure 6-3: A decision-making graphic organizer for an O. Henry short story

Questions for "After Twenty Years"

1. Would you remember an appointment after 20 years?

2. Would you betray a friend if it cost you your job if you didn't?

3. Would you pretend you did not know your friend so that you would not have to confront him?

4. Would you get someone else to turn in your friend?

5. Would you tell your friend that he is wanted by the law and give him a chance to turn himself in?

6. If he would not turn himself in, would you give him a chance to run?

Relevance means that we also help students to make sense of the learning by teaching to the modality that is most comfortable to them. Most of what students learn in school comes to them through auditory, visual, or kinesthetic senses. We have already stated that most learners are visual (need to see the learning), auditory (need to hear the learning and repeat it to themselves), or kinesthetic (need to do something with the learning). Most children of poverty are a combination of visual and kinesthetic. Some teachers will say that they teach primarily by lecture and that the better, more motivated students "get it" and only those students who don't care don't get it. Students with high intrinsic motivation usually are good adapters; they adapt to the modality used by their teachers. However, students who struggle, who don't grab the new learning easily, must be retaught in the modality most comfortable to their brain wiring if they are ever going to "get it" (Jensen, 2004). Reteaching in the same modality will get the same results it got the first time. If educators could find more ways to show kids how math works, we would raise math scores all over this country—for all kids. For 87% of the students in any given classroom, just memorizing formulas is not enough; they need to see how the formula works (Jensen, 2004).

Rigor

As we stated in chapter 1, every child deserves a rigorous, quality education. No one deserves a watered-down curriculum. To give students a mediocre education is to assure them a life of low-paying jobs. Once, in a training session, a teacher asked us during the break, "I think this information is great, but the truth is that if we educate everyone to the fullest, who will clean hotel rooms or work in restaurants?" Once we overcame our initial shock that anyone in this day and time held that opinion, we responded, "Casualties are light unless you are one of them. Who will the failure be—your kid, my kid?" We cannot afford to have *any* casualties in education. Why would we want to set any child up for failure?

According to Jensen (2004), the best learning state is one in which students are moderately challenged, so that they remain motivated. We do not want the challenge to be impossible; we want it to be incremental. An important piece of motivation is self-efficacy. Self-efficacy is different from self-esteem. Self-esteem says, "I feel good about myself, and I believe I can do this," while self-efficacy says, "I know I can do this because I have been successful before." Self-efficacy is stronger than self-esteem, because it is built on fact, while self-esteem is built on thoughts and feelings.

In trying to make students feel good about themselves or to build self-efficacy, we must not make the mistake of "watering down the learning." Students know when they are being given an inferior curriculum or when their work is not the same as others in the classroom. No child deserves to get an inferior education; every child deserves to learn at a high level. If we are teaching to standards (not below them) and if we are utilizing relevancy, we will be teaching to rigor and offering the kind of challenge that motivates students and increases self-efficacy.

Scaffolding the Learning

How, you might ask, can we teach with high rigor to students who come to us with gaps in learning? How can we get them to high-level thinking when they are struggling with basic understanding? A good analogy for how we do this lies in the architecture of buildings. Look at a skyscraper going up in your area. Can you walk on the upper floors of the building before the structure is in place? No, of course not—you would fall if you tried. However, scaffolding allows workers to move to higher levels to work even before the building is completed. Once the upper floors are in place, the scaffolding is removed as it is no longer needed for access to the higher floors of the building. The same principle is applied to raising the learning level of students in the classroom. By providing the scaffolding, we create a way for students to gain the understanding needed to venture to higher learning.

How scaffolding works. In Mr. Graham's class, students are working on math problems. Mr. Graham has provided scaffolding in the form of logarithms that they must follow if they are going to get the correct answer. Heuristics are the general rules that students follow when they are not required to get the same answer every time (for example, the general rules used to set up mindmaps). In this case, there is only one right answer to each of the problems, so Mr. Graham provides the step-by-step rules in writing. When students are having difficulty with the problems, the first thing that Mr. Graham does is to ask the students to look at the rules and see if they have followed the step-by-step process.

Mrs. Anderson's class is creating timelines. Prior to making the assignment, Mrs. Anderson provided the students with a rubric that listed the important parts of a timeline and the attributes that made each part of the essay high quality. Here is an example of the rubric that Mrs. Anderson provided for her class:

- Is the title prominent and concise?

- Are the lines ruled, and are the events placed on the line correctly?

- Are the time elements uniform in size, easy to read, correct, and at equal intervals with subheadings in between?

- Are the labels uniform in size, legible, and clearly indicating the important events?

• Are the illustrations appropriate?

• Are the credits discrete and alphabetized?

• Is the overall appearance neat and legible?

By providing this rubric in detail, Mrs. Anderson is providing scaffolding for her students so that they know what the component parts are and what they look like if they are completed at a high level.

Mr. Garcia's class does pretty well on the math work that they are learning this week, but two weeks from now they will struggle with questions or problems on that same math work when it is given for review. To help his students keep the many formulas and math examples straight, he provides them with a graph like the one in Table 6-2 for keeping their math strategies for the year.

Table 6-2: Math Strategies

Math concept	Steps	Example	How will I know if it is correct?	My notes

As you can see, scaffolding is simply providing students with everything that they need to be successful. We want students to be aware of the types of scaffolding we are giving them so that they can provide their own scaffolding in the future. The goal is to take away the scaffolding as students grow in their ability to learn and to understand how they learned.

Some other examples of the way that we provide scaffolding include the following:

1. Teaching the vocabulary of the lessons up front

2. Creating good formative assessments that help students to identify areas of weakness and to improve

3. Assessing exactly what is taught—no "gotchas"

4. Making sure that our students have the basic skills in place before moving to high-level skills, or else providing the rules and examples of the basic skills in advance

5. Using rubrics that are specific

6. Adequately teaching concepts before assessing them or giving homework in them

7. Providing backups to our lessons through podcasts, online, help, or written directions

Stimulating In-Depth Thinking

A guiding principle when providing rigor is to ensure that your students know and understand the content at an in-depth level. The work of Grant Wiggins and Jay McTighe (2001, 2005) provides one of the best ways to look at the level of understanding. Using their six guidelines for understanding, we can lead our students to more complex thinking by cultivating in them the following skills:

1. **The ability to explain the learning in the student's own words**—When students can explain things in their own terms, they are also demonstrating that the information has become relevant. Students who can explain can also justify, predict, and prove.

2. **The ability to interpret the learning**—This requires that students can document, evaluate, and make sense of the information. They should also be able to tell a story about the information. Daniel Pink's *A Whole New Mind* (2005) tells us that most of the world learns in a story format rather than in the linear a, b, c listings that we so often use in our classrooms, and that one attribute needed by those who would be successful is the ability to explain something in a story format. This is a part of interpreting the learning and providing context to the information.

3. **The ability to apply the learning in a context other than the one in which it was learned**—Students may be able to apply a mathematical principle to the classroom work, but can they apply that same principle to a real-world problem? If students can apply, they can adapt, use, and design.

4. **The ability to see things in perspective**—If students can put information into perspective, they can analyze it, make inferences, and compare and contrast. For example, students studying the Lincoln-Douglas debate can examine the two people involved in the debate in terms of how they were alike, how they were different, and how their personal attributes shaped their thinking and comments in the debate.

5. **The ability to empathize**—This is a very complex task, because it requires that students look at issues from another's perspective, not just their own. It does not mean agreeing with the other perspective; it means understanding why the other person feels as he or she does. Seeing another's point of view is also one of Daniel Pink's important "senses" for the 21st century.

6. **The ability to know ourselves and be honest about that appraisal**—This requires the ability to reflect and self-assess. Often students from poverty have a low locus of control; they may believe that they do not control who or what they are.

At a minimum, all students—and especially students who are from poverty—should be directly taught these six levels of understanding.

Curriculum Calibration

Students' work should at least meet the level of understanding of the standards and benchmarks for their grade level. As a teacher, can you walk the objectives of the classroom back to the specific standard and benchmark, and does the level of work in the classroom meet the level of understanding required in the standard?

For example, a benchmark found in all state standards requires that students "know the defining characteristics of a variety of genres" (and then lists the genres for the grade level). If I am teaching genres in my classroom, just having students memorize the types of genres and definitions is not adequate. It does not meet the understanding level of the benchmark. Notice that the benchmark says students will know the "defining characteristics." If I know the defining characteristics of something, I know what makes it uniquely what it is, rather than something else. I may know the definition of a tall tale, but unless I know the characteristics that make it a tall tale instead of a fantasy, I have not met the rigor of the standard. Make sure that you have identified what the standard is asking of the students and that the rigor is identified as well.

Relationships

For many students from poverty, relationships take precedence over almost everything else. It is the one thing that gives them ownership. When differentiating for content, it is important to note that first we must build a relationship with students that has as its premise that we are all learners together—including the teacher. It is not the curriculum and the teacher against the student; it is the teacher and student together tackling the curriculum, and together they will be successful.

* * * * *

Teaching, like sculpture, is both art and a science. Michelangelo was arguably the most gifted sculptor in history, and the magnificence of his creations could never be imitated using mechanical means. Yet even this brilliant artist studied his craft. He worked not only on the methods and materials necessary to create his works of art, he also studied anatomy—learning the structure and connections of the bodies he later created in stone. Even the most gifted among us will profit from learning the structure, the composition, and the "hows" and "whys" of our art—teaching. We need to look to science to answer questions about the structure and function of the human brain. We need to understand how learning actually happens and reflect on how research can be applied in our own unique circumstances. We need to do our best, because what we do matters (Spangler, 2001).

Differentiating Product

Products are the evidence provided by our students that they know and understand the learning. These products demonstrate the depth of their mastery. As a general rule, start where students are, and guide them to where you want them to be. You know where your students are in terms of understanding and being able to effectively use the learning through observation, formative assessments, individual and group discussion, and analyzing available data. Ask yourself, "At this grade level, what is the expected depth of understanding?" State standards and benchmarks or learning indicators can help with this. These indicators show you the state expectations for all students by grade level and subject area. Your school may also have standards that indicate the expectation for both the school district and individual schools. For example, an indicator may say that by grade 6, students can identify the characteristics of various genres (tall tale, myth, fantasy, science fiction, poem, and so on). If students are reading two grade levels below their actual classroom grade level, how can a teacher make informed decisions about meeting this indicator? The first step will be to identify where the students are now. Do they know the vocabulary words *tall tale, myth,* and so on? Do they know the critical attributes of each of those genres? If they read a myth, would they know why it was a myth instead of a fantasy? The products produced by students may be very simple at first—they may be on a knowledge and comprehension basis. That is all right, because we know that they must master a product at that level before we can expect them to be able to analyze their work. Beginning-level products might include the following:

- Creation of a word chart that demonstrates that the student knows the word (*genre, tall tale,* and so on) and can define it

- Completion of an attribute wheel that shows the student knows the various attributes of the individual genres and can demonstrate why a fantasy is a fantasy instead of a tall tale

- Creation of a compare-and-contrast chart that shows how a fantasy is *different* from a tall tale

Now we have moved our students into a fairly complex task that requires them to know the words, understand them, be able to analyze what makes them uniquely what they are, and then synthesize that information into a compare and contrast.

From the Simple to the Complex: Bloom's Taxonomy

As a general rule, we use Bloom's Taxonomy (1956) as our guide to moving students from the simple to the complex. Please note that we did not say to move students from *easy* to *difficult.* You can provide students with low-level work that is difficult and time-consuming; you can also provide them with high-level work that is easy for them. The goal is to move students from simple tasks such as making a timeline (something students can do without understanding the information itself) to evaluating decisions made along the timeline and their influence on it (a task that requires analysis, synthesis, and evaluation).

Let's take a closer look at possible student products based on Bloom's Taxonomy.

Knowledge

Students know the information provided and can recall it in the form that it was presented, as in the following examples:

- Can recall a definition provided by the teacher regardless of whether the definition makes sense to the learner

- Can draw a timeline of the invention of the chronometer

- Can memorize written definitions or other pieces of information in the format given in the classroom (for example, 4 x 4 = 16)

- Can create a 25-fact card file on Balboa

Comprehension

The student understands the information and can provide an explanation in his or her own words. O'Tuel and Bullard (1993) say that students who can translate a math problem into a verbal problem are demonstrating this level of the taxonomy, as in the following examples:

- Can write a want ad for a Romantic hero using information from the Romantic Period in literature
- Can write definitions in their own words, using the word chart for teaching vocabulary
- Can explain why 4 x 4 is always 16

Application

Students know the information and understand it, so that they can apply it to contexts other than the ones given by the teacher, as follows:

- Can organize the vocabulary words into categories
- Can construct a model of a cell
- Can explain the concept to a new student who missed the class
- Can use graphics
- Can apply the information to a real-world context

Analysis

As mentioned in an earlier book on special learners (Tileston, 2004c), analysis requires higher-level thinking. For our students from poverty and diverse learners, it means they are able to do the following:

- Can break information apart or into categories; they can analyze information, compare it and look at the organizational sets

- Can isolate the important attributes that will be necessary to understand why two genres are different

- Can compare and contrast an amphibian and a reptile

- Can debate an issue we have discussed

Synthesis

O'Tuel and Bullard (1993) say that synthesis "includes the ability to organize, to arrange elements into meaningful relationships and to make inferences about those relationships. When students write compositions, regardless of the type, they are creating something new based on what they know" (p. 20). Much of synthesis relies on analysis, as in the following examples of student proficiency:

- Can compose a rap song to help remember a concept

- Can predict the ending of the story based on the facts the student has so far

- Can create a hypothesis for an experiment based on what the student knows about the elements

- Can create a new ending to the story using the elements of good storytelling

Evaluation

The student has the ability to make judgments based on fact, as in the following:

- Can defend beliefs about the ethics of transplanting embryonic tissue to save lives

- Can justify his or her decision regarding whether the argument provided in the book *Earrings!* by Judith Viorst is valid

- Can rate his or her decisions

Table 6-3: Type of Product Based on Level of Complexity

Level of Bloom's	Topic of Product to Be Submitted by Student	Final Product
Knowledge		
Label	Parts of the brain	Sketch
List	Freedoms in the Bill of Rights	Chart
Identify	Parts of a plant	Model
Comprehension		
Explain	How to perform a math operation	Email
Summarize	The events that led to the fall of Hitler	Graphic organizer
Discuss	The importance of nature to the Romantic Period in literature	Essay
Application		
Demonstrate	A daily task performed by the colonists	Demonstration
Construct	A model of the brain	Model
Classify	Information as fact or fiction	Lesson
Analysis		
Compare and Contrast	The Pilgrims' stories in *The Canterbury Tales* to the stories told by the people who frequented the *Cheers* television show	Compare/Contrast
Diagram		Chart
		Diagram
Synthesis		
Predict	The importance of technology to the future	Letter to the editor
Invent	A way to help you remember vocabulary words	Teach
Evaluation		
Criticize	The policies on the *Titanic* regarding telegrams that led to its sinking	Debate

Used with permission (Tileston, 2004c).

Rubrics

Lastly, it is critical to provide students with a rubric for any-thing that will be assessed, whether it is homework or individual projects. Why? Because students do not come to us knowing what a quality product is unless we show them and provide a measurement that explicitly tells them the expectation. Always give the rubric "up front" when the assignment is made and always make it very spe-cific. When you do this, you not only teach students what is meant by *quality products,* you also take the "gotcha" out of the assessment. If students do the work according to the criteria provided, they get the grade. If the work falls below the expectation, they know where the problem is and what they need to do to fix it. Table 6-4 is an example of a matrix for a persuasive essay.

Table 6-4: Matrix for a Persuasive Essay

Parts (Essentials)	Points	Attributes (Qualities)
Thesis statement		Takes clear position
		Logical
Introduction		Grabs attention
		Last sentence contains thesis statement
Voice		Targets intended audience
Reasons		Topic sentence(s) state three reasons clearly
		Emotion/logic based
Support/elaboration		Uses transition statements as links
		Is supported by examples/other elaboration techniques
		Contains clinchers
Conclusions		Restates position statement
		Reestablishes reasons
		Includes call to action

Summary of Chapter Six

In this chapter we have discussed ways to provide relevant and meaningful content that leads to rigorous learning and quality products from our students: Begin with students where they are, and lead them up the complexity of Bloom's Taxonomy one step at a time. Assess them consistently and fairly by providing the criteria for success in advance and using that criteria for both formative and summative evaluations. Take the "gotcha" out of the learning. Make all students' talents marketable by ensuring that they are exposed to relevance (real-world and personal) and rigor (depth of understanding). Demonstrate daily your belief that every student deserves a quality education.

CHAPTER SEVEN

Differentiating Process

Brain research confirms what experienced teachers have always known:

No two children are alike.

No two children learn in the identical way.

An enriched environment for one student is not necessarily enriched for another.

In the classroom we should teach children to think for themselves.

—Marian Diamond

Poverty has been studied and analyzed for years. The results are in: poverty changes brains.

—Eric Jensen

One of the most significant ways in which teachers can differentiate instruction for children of poverty is by modifying the *processes* of learning—the ways they provide students with experiences and opportunities for processing information so that they can *make their own meaning* out of the content. By differentiating process, we can integrate what we know about the needs of these students.

To better understand how to differentiate process, we find it helpful to understand how the brain processes the learning tasks that we, as teachers, put before our students. There are many models of how the brain takes in, stores, and retrieves information. However, the one we find the most useful is Marzano's *Systems of Thinking* (1998). Its purpose is to find "categories specific and functional enough to provide guidance for classroom instruction" (p. 10). As shown in Figure 7-1, the systems of thinking consist of three categories, which are engaged in a specific order by the brain: the *self system*, the *metacognitive system*, and the *cognitive system*.

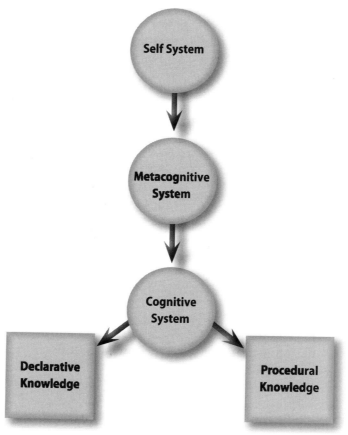

Figure 7-1: An outline of Marzano's systems of thinking, derived from Marzano (1998)

The Self System—Do I Want to Do It?

When teachers initially present their students with a learning task, the student's brain first engages the self system to ask the following:

- "Do I want to do this?"

- "How important is this to *me?*"

- "Will I be successful at this learning task?"

All students ask these questions, consciously or unconsciously. The significance for students from poverty and diverse cultures is that they are more likely to answer "no" to all them. Why? For many, the learning presented in their classrooms lacks personal meaning, because mainstream middle-class education typically does not relate to collectivist cultures. Students from poverty are also more likely to have had negative experiences with past learning and to lack the belief that they can be successful. If these students determine the answer to be no, learning does not occur for them. Whether they answer yes or no, whether they will want to learn, depends on the following subcategories of Marzano's self system:

- **Self attributes**—Their beliefs about themselves relative to accomplishing the task

- **Self and others**—Their perceptions about themselves in relation to others

- **Worldview**—Their values and beliefs about the overall nature of the world

- **Purpose**—Their perception of their purpose in the world

- **Self-efficacy**—Their belief about whether they can or can't succeed with the task at hand

The self system is the control center for thinking and action. Teachers who use instructional strategies that have an impact on the self system produce powerful results—a gain of as much as 31 percentile points in achievement (Marzano, 1998)!

The Metacognitive System—How Will I Do It?

Let's assume the teacher has presented a learning task, and the self system is engaged: The student *wants* to perform the learning task, is *motivated* to learn it, and *believes* he or she can learn it. Now the metacognitive system is engaged, and the student's brain asks these questions:

- "What are my goals?"
- "How will I learn best?"
- "What strategies do I need to use to achieve my goals?"
- "How will I monitor my learning so I know I'm achieving my goals?"

If students cannot set a goal to accomplish the learning task, don't know how they learn, don't have any strategies from their past to call upon, and have no way to monitor their learning along the way, they will be overwhelmed, and very little learning will occur. Without these resources, a sense of hopelessness sets in and children quit, sometimes announcing, "This is too hard! I can't do it." Or they blame the learning task itself. You may have heard in your classroom, "This is so dumb! Why do we have to do this?" These are defense mechanisms children use when they don't know how to set goals, form a plan, and then execute the plan to accomplish the task.

The metacognitive system in the brain contains information about the nature and importance of plans, timelines, and resources, as well as strategies for accomplishing goals. It has three subcategories:

1. **Goal specification**—Planning and setting goals

2. **Process specification and monitoring**–Feedback and information relative to the *strategies* used to accomplish their goals

3. **Disposition monitoring**–Feedback on how one is doing with the task or goal

The metacognitive system is the engine of learning. Instructional techniques used by teachers that have an impact on the metacognitive system produce powerful results—a gain of as much as 26 percentile points in achievement (Marzano, 1998).

The Cognitive System—How Will I Make Meaning Out of It?

The cognitive system is responsible for the *effective processing* of the information necessary for learning. As much as you might want to, you cannot get your students to engage in effective processing if they disengage in thinking before their brain gets to this stage. Regardless of where you begin the lesson, learning will proceed from the self system to the metacognitive system, and only then to the cognitive system. If you start class by going right to the substance of the lesson, students may miss part of the information while they are going through the process of deciding if it is personally relevant, whether they want to pay attention, and so on. That is why we recommend that you begin with the self system.

Let's assume that you've presented your students with a learning task and that they've already successfully engaged both the self and the metacognitive systems. The cognitive system now asks the following:

- "What learning strategies do I know for this task?"

- "What parts of this task do I already know how to do?"

- "How is this task similar or different from another task I know?"

- "What information do I need to learn this task? What skills do I need to learn and refine?"

When the cognitive system is engaged, it interacts with the two knowledge domains—declarative knowledge, which consists of information; and procedural knowledge, which consists of skills and processes. Almost every state standard, goal, and objective of the expected learning for students is in the knowledge domains. If the cognitive system remains successfully engaged, students will be successful in learning.

The Impact of Systems of Thinking on Diverse Learners

Because most teachers are Euro-American and from middle-class backgrounds, they may be unaware of the needs of students from diverse cultures and children of poverty in terms of engaging them in learning. Many of these children come to your classroom with unique needs that affect their learning and must guide your teaching. These include the following:

- **The significance of relationships**—Relationships are important in Mexican American, African American, Native American, Arabic, Asian, and other collectivist cultures.

- **Self-efficacy**—Their academic self-concept is low.

- **Planning**—Many Mexican American and African American children need assistance with goal-setting, organizational skills, and prioritizing.

- **Problem-solving**—For these children, issues used for problem-solving need to be relevant to the culture. They first ask the question, "How will this help me personally to reach a goal, solve a problem, or make my life better?

- **Locus of control**—When the expectations at school do not match expectations from their homes and the community, and when those expectations are not explicitly taught, students can feel they don't have control over anything in their lives. This is especially true of any students who may be living with violence at home; children who live with violence have a lowered locus of control, because they cannot control the constant threat to their lives. They assume then that a force larger than themselves controls what happens to them, and that they do not have choices.

- **Ability to trust people and systems**—Children from generational poverty, from families whose culture is not valued or respected, and children whose parents were unsuccessful in school, come to school wary, unsure of whether the people and school can be trusted.

- **Response to criticism**—Mexican American children in particular are often sensitive to criticism by teachers and elders in their community.

- **Vocabulary**—On average, poor children of color come to school with half the vocabulary of white, middle-class children (Marzano, 2003).

- **Prior knowledge and experience**—Poor children of color tend to have different prior knowledge and experiences than Euro-American children. And since they also have fewer vocabulary words, they have difficulty expressing that prior knowledge and experience.

How can we use what we know about the systems of thinking and the needs of children of poverty and diverse cultures to differentiate instruction in order to meet their needs? First, we need to remember when we design our units and lesson plans that learning tasks require the brain to engage *all* of its systems of thinking. Then we need to plan strategies to do this.

Teachers can create proficient instruction that appreciates cultural references and takes into account the social conditions and hardships that many children of poverty face. When they do so—when they include students' cultural and social experiences as a means to implement best practices and develop new knowledge—learning becomes more significant to these children. When teachers understand resilience and exhibit teacher behaviors that demonstrate high expectations, when they consider social dynamics and use diverse teaching methods, students will be successful with the learning tasks demanded by state standards.

Let's look at some of the instructional strategies that teachers can use to overcome the "pedagogy of poverty," in which low-level tasks dominate instruction and learning opportunities (Haberman, 1991).

Self-System Strategies

As we pointed out earlier, when you introduce students to a learning task, the self system engages first. Many children of poverty, however, are not intrinsically motivated by learning tasks and do not believe they will be successful at them. What instructional strategies can teachers use to get students to decide, "I want to learn. I *can* learn that. Learning that is important to me!"? These strategies include explicit feedback, cooperative learning, praise, and relevance.

Explicit Feedback

Explicit feedback has a great impact on students' self-perception, both as learners and as people. A child's self-perception as a learner is most often set in first grade. Children know that first grade is when they are expected to learn to read. They're not sure about what else is expected, but learning to read is a given. However, when children of poverty struggle with learning to read, they often decide that they are not readers or learners—that reading is just too hard. They give up and focus their energies on other things, like being funny or distracting others. Our experiences with children of poverty have shown us that without an intervention by a trusted adult working to alter that perception in the self system, the child will give up. Explicit feedback can result in as much as a 37 percentile point gain in achievement (Darling, 1999). But the feedback must be explicit. That is to say, it must have these qualities:

- It is descriptive—It describes the work submitted in detail.

- It is informative—It includes what the student can reflect on that will add to his or her understanding.

- It is specific—It lets the student know exactly what was great, what was okay, and what needs further work.

- It is guiding—It tells students what corrective action should be taken and what should be continued.

Explicit feedback is *not* simply a comment such as "Good job" or "Nice work," which doesn't say *why* it is a good job or nice work or contain information about what to do next. And it is not just words of encouragement like "Keep up the good work"—although encouragement *with* explicit feedback is a great combination.

Cooperative Learning

Cooperative learning can increase learning by as much as 28 percentile points, particularly when used with the model developed by Roger and David Johnson of the Cooperative Learning Center at the University of Minnesota (Darling, 1999). Cooperative learning has a significant impact on the student's perception of self and others. Another benefit of Johnson and Johnson's model is that it supports students' awareness and acceptance of differences among themselves, as well as their perception of themselves as persons and as learners. Remember, too, that students from cultures with collectivist value systems especially benefit from the opportunity to work together.

Praise

Praising the effort that students put into their work, even if the product isn't perfect, can create a 29 percentile point gain in achievement (Darling, 1999) and affects students' sense of efficacy. We can support children of poverty in believing that they are valued members of the classroom and can learn. All of these strategies have an impact on developing resilience in and relationships with children, factors that are critical in overcoming the effects of poverty on learning (Williams, 2003). Creating a trusting relationship between teachers and students must precede effective teaching and learning. Werner & Smith (1992) write, "The resilient youngsters in our study all had at least one person in their lives who accepted them unconditionally, regardless of temperamental idiosyncrasies, physical attractiveness, or intelligence" (p. 205).

Relevance

We are all born into this world hardwired to learn and be curious. If you don't believe us, watch any 2-year-old. Children this age are constantly "into things," using their hands and mouths and senses to explore the world. Similarly, when introducing a new piece of learning in the classroom, engage your students' curiosity on many fronts: Use novelty, challenges, unique hooks to the content, and other brain-compatible ways to jumpstart thinking and engage the self system. For children of poverty from diverse cultures, it is critical to make the learning task responsive to their cultures. Many African American and Latino children of poverty need to see and hear examples that reflect their culture. Remember, while poverty has a negative impact on academic achievement, it is not the only factor that affects learning. White children of poverty in California outperformed African American and Latino children who were *not* poor on the STAR tests released in August, 2007 (Mangaliman, 2007).

If teachers use culturally responsive, relevant tasks to engage the brain's self system, the resulting response will be more students choosing to engage and fewer students who choose to tune out and drop out. Seek ways to show students from poverty how the lesson will help them in some way—how it applies to their lives right now. Remember that many children of poverty live only in the here and now. They may not be interested in the fact that what they are learning today will be useful in high school or college. They want to know, "What will this do for me now?"

Metacognitive System Strategies

The second system that a student's brain engages is the metacognitive system—the engine of learning. The unique needs of many children of color and students living in poverty have a huge impact on the metacognitive system. They have difficulty planning and setting reasonable goals and priorities, and often they don't know how to estimate how long a task will take. These children need to bring forward prior learning and experiences to assist them with the goal of learning what teachers are asking of them today. Their experiences and prior knowledge may be dramatically different than those of middle-class students. As a result, some learning tasks may overwhelm them even before they begin—especially if the task has an additional part, such as using the writing process. How can teachers assist students in successfully transitioning through the metacognitive system and in building resilience that they can draw upon the next time they encounter a different learning task?

Specific Learning Objectives

Provide students with specific learning objectives before starting a lesson. The specificity with which you present these objectives determines the impact they will have on student achievement. Goal-setting will impact learning by 34 percentile points (Darling, 1999) if teachers provide the scaffolding for students to achieve it. In addition, allowing students to have some control over the design of the learning outcomes can increase learning by 39 percentile points (Darling, 1999).

Self-Talk and Verbalization

Teachers can also teach, model, and reinforce for students how to prioritize learning tasks using self-talk and verbalization. Ruby Payne (2001) refers to this as "procedural self-talk," and it helps children of poverty break down the tasks of a project into doable steps. Students write down their responses to describe the steps they will take to accomplish a project until they reach a point where they understand how they can accomplish the task. They "internalize completion" in the process. Self-talk is similar to a powerful instructional strategy called *verbalization,* in which students "think aloud." In verbalization, teachers encourage learners to express the learning and connection-making process aloud to themselves and others. Verbalizing both thinking and processing enables students to both "listen" to and "hear" their thought processes aloud and provides dual encoding to the brain. Verbalization enables students to do the following:

- Talk aloud to each other about what they know and how it relates to the new ideas the learning task presents them. This helps them activate prior knowledge and build cognitive frameworks for new ideas, concepts, and principles.

- Assimilate and conceptualize new information about what they are learning as they listen to new information. Students listen to new information presented by the teacher or their group, then, reflecting the brain's processing of the new information, verbalize their understanding of what they have heard to the teacher or their group.

- Verbalize their ideas, hypotheses, and logic as they reason aloud with each other. This helps them create links between informal, intuitive notions and logical steps, abstract language, and symbolism. They "hear" themselves expressing their thinking, which helps them to better understand their ideas, logic, and reasoning.

- Monitor and verbalize their own mental activity. This develops in students an awareness of the way in which their minds work (metacognition); that is, it strengthens their ability to think about thinking.

Verbalization can produce as much as a 46 percentile point gain in learning (Darling, 1999)!

In many traditional classrooms, we encourage students to think silently and work alone (a Euro-American individualistic value). But the benefits of the very quiet classroom and silent thinking are not worth the loss of opportunities to learn. Verbalization is a strategy applicable to all grades and all subjects, from kindergarten through grade 12.

When encouraging verbalization, teachers can provide an environment that encourages voiced thinking while at the same time monitoring the execution of complex tasks. Teachers can enhance the discussion by consistently providing input that stimulates problem-solving, question-raising, formulation of conjectures, presentation of solutions, and determination of validity. Teachers should also encourage students who are exploring and sharing their understanding of new ideas and concepts to use invented terms and symbols, analogies, metaphors, stories, written hypotheses, explanations, arguments, oral presentations, and dramatizations.

Wait Time

Another strategy that affects children's ability to monitor how they are doing is *wait time*. (We looked at this strategy briefly in the checklist for culturally relevant classrooms on page 64.) Many children of poverty, as well as diverse learners from collectivist cultures and English-language learners, need extra time to think. When teachers ask questions without giving these children sufficient processing time before they call on someone else to answer, they unwittingly contribute to the students' feelings of helplessness. Students who can't answer quickly wonder, "Why bother to even try?" After a while, they conclude, "Why even listen to the question?!" Teachers should mentally count to 10 before asking for a response either chorally or from an individual student. Some teachers use a hand signal after the wait time is up to cue students that they may now respond.

Activating Prior Knowledge

Activating prior knowledge, a strategy that we have discussed frequently in this book, uses storage and retrieval procedures, such as anticipation guides and KNLH plus, that are designed to elicit preconceived ideas, retrieve known knowledge, and provide a focus for the new information. This strategy provides students with ways to store and recall information through all five pathways to memory:

1. Semantic (based on words)

2. Episodic (based on location)

3. Procedural (based on movement and manipulating objects)

4. Automatic (based on procedure without conscious thought)

5. Emotional (based on emotions)

Using nonlinguistic organizers that assist students in storing and retrieving information is a powerful means of embedding and retrieving information. Done in a cooperative learning group, it is even more effective for diverse learners and children of poverty. Activating prior knowledge enables students to do the following:

- Restructure the learning task by connecting it to a real-life example from their own experience.

- Record the results of their retrieved information using concept maps, graphic outlines, and advance organizers.

- Make connections between new and known knowledge.

Activating prior knowledge can be used at the beginning of, during, or at the end of a lesson to increase academic achievement for children of poverty by a whopping 46 percentile points (Darling, 1999).

Creating Scaffolding

Scaffolding the learning can help to level the playing field. Sometimes the scaffold takes the form of providing background knowledge through the use of a conceptual framework like a graphic organizer to give students a base on which to make meaningful connections. For children of poverty from diverse cultures, it is important that the context for that background knowledge also be responsive to the cultures represented in the classroom. Scaffolding means providing learning support for the student and gradually removing that support as the student exhibits the ability to handle the task independently. Scaffolding is critical to the success of students with minimal experience with new learning tasks, especially if they are complex. For a detailed look at scaffolding with examples, see p. 97 in chapter 6, "Differentiating Content and Product."

Preteaching Vocabulary

We know that often children of poverty come to us with fewer words in their vocabulary. Preteaching the vocabulary for your learning task, again using a nonlinguistic organizer for students to record their meaning, will level the playing field when instruction on the content begins. Using an effective strategy to preteach vocabulary can increase learning by as much as 49 percentile points (Darling, 1999). See chapter 4, "Planning to Differentiate," for a more detailed look at preteaching vocabulary.

* * * * *

These research-based strategies will help students develop a plan for learning, understand what a reasonable time expectation is for each part of the task, assist them in organizing and prioritizing, help them to connect the new learning to prior experience and knowledge, and increase the likelihood that they will undertake the task with a realistic game plan for completing it. Using these tools to engage the metacognitive system, you can eliminate the sense of helplessness and the feeling of being overwhelmed by the learning task that many children of poverty experience. They can then go on to safely engage the cognitive system.

Cognitive System Strategies

In the cognitive system, students process information from the learning task to make their own meaning and to embed the new learning into memory. Students use strategies from the cognitive system to learn the objectives of your well-designed, differentiated lessons and to focus on the expectations of your state's standards. What you want your students to know (declarative knowledge) and be able to do (procedural knowledge) as a result of their learning drives the strategies that they will choose. However, you can help them to choose wisely. There are four subcategories of the cognitive system that your students use, depending on the objectives of the lesson:

- Storage and retrieval—Used for storing and retrieving information like math facts, formulas, and steps in a process
- Information processing—Used to demonstrate the learning through comparing, categorizing, analyzing, or synthesizing
- Input/output communication processes—Used when students engage in reading, writing, speaking, and listening
- Knowledge utilization processes—Used to solve problems, conduct an inquiry, make a decision, and investigate

Storage and Retrieval Strategies

Learning the declarative knowledge of state standards in any subject is almost always a storage and retrieval process. Let's look closer at three of these strategies—activating prior knowledge, cues, and questioning.

Activating Prior Knowledge

Activating prior knowledge is a powerful strategy used before, during, and after learning that has an impact on both the metacognitive and cognitive systems, and is used before, during, and after instruction. Activating prior knowledge can increase learning by 46 percentile points (Darling, 1999).

Cues

When you provide a brief preview of the information or skills students are going to address, you are providing cues to the new learning. Use verbal cues to prompt students for retrieval of information. Use them also to elicit prior knowledge or experience, to remind students of a mnemonic or vocabulary word learned or of a known pattern, or to prompt them to "think aloud" (verbalization). When students give the correct response to a cue, acknowledge the strategy they used and their persistence and give praise. Providing students with cues can raise achievement by 37 percentile points (Darling, 1999).

Questioning Strategies

Questioning strategies used by teachers are another way to help students retrieve information. Effective questioning strategies can raise achievement by 32 percentile points (Darling, 1999). A word of caution, however: Be sure to ask questions of your children of poverty at all levels of Bloom's Taxonomy. They can and will respond to analysis, synthesis, and evaluation questions that are *relevant* to their experiences. For example, after they have been pretaught the vocabulary they need to use, ask students to use a graphic organizer to compare the theme of Shakespeare's *Romeo and Juliet* against their own life experiences; they can reinforce relationships in pairs or small groups in which they can "think aloud," and have an opportunity to participate and contribute. This is doubly significant for children of poverty from diverse cultures.

Information Processing

Information processing requires the brain to *do* something with the information students have acquired and includes the following.

Compare and Contrast

Comparing and contrasting requires students to identify the similarities and differences between two or more things. Some graphic organizers, like T-charts and Venn diagrams, can show students not only what the critical attributes of a topic are, but also what they are not. Providing examples and nonexamples of a topic also requires students' brains to compare and contrast. Allow your students to work with these organizers in groups. Compare and contrast can raise achievement by 40 percentile points (Darling, 1999) and can be even more powerful if students create analogies linking new with known content in unique ways. Joyce & Weil's synectics is a strategy from their *Models of Teaching* (2000) that uses analogies. Use this powerful method for stimulating creative thinking and writing when you want students to "think outside the box." Creating analogies to link new content with known content can create a 45 percentile point gain in achievement (Darling, 1999).

Graphic Representations

How do graphic representations specifically aid the processing of information? Graphic representations like semantic maps and Venn diagrams give information a pattern, which supports better understanding and meaning making, and are a powerful strategy for children of poverty and diverse cultures. The brain loves patterns! These representations enable learners to do the following:

- Organize main ideas and key concepts, causal relations, vocabulary, symbols, principles, and generalizations.

- Plan the sequence of their work, represent hierarchical information, organize sources of information, and record the brainstorming efforts of cooperative teams.

- Represent the connections between new knowledge and prior knowledge.

- Process new learning into long-term memory.

When using graphic representations, prepare and teach the organizing and representational framework that you are using first. Then prompt students on the content being represented and organized, such as various kinds of relationships, new knowledge and prior knowledge, concepts and connecting ideas, main idea and subordinate details, process sequences, and so on. This strategy can increase learning by as much as 49 percentile points (Darling, 1999). Care needs to be taken by teachers to choose the graphic organizers carefully, with regard to the objectives of the lesson.

Active Teaching

Good (1983) defined active teaching as teaching that is responsive to students' needs and interests. It can take a number of forms. Darling-Hammond (2000) emphasizes the importance of teachers being able to be proficient at a number of teaching practices in order to have an impact on student learning. Through an understanding of Gardner's multiple intelligences (1999) and applications to teaching like Carol Ann Tomlinson's (1999) differentiated instructional practices and the Learning Bridges Model for Differentiation, teachers have the capacity to meet the needs of their children of poverty.

Manipulatives

This strategy has been well received in elementary schools and can increase learning by 31 percentile points (Darling, 1999). Manipulatives require the physical manipulation of concrete or symbolic artifacts. In the digital age, it is interesting to note that the use of computer simulation to manipulate artifacts (compared to physically manipulating objects) produced the highest impact on learning—43 percentile points (Darling, 1999). An example of this is a computer simulation for teaching slides, transformation, rotations, geometric shapes in mathematics, and so on.

Information Specification and Generalization

Generalization requires students to *infer generalizations* from observations or specific pieces of information—in other words, to engage in inductive thinking. Specification requires students to *make predictions* based on known generalizations or principles. We teach generalization when we want students to classify and identify a label for that classification. Students infer the generalization from the examples to be classified. An example might be making predictions about items included in a category.

Input/Output Communication Processes

Many studies have been conducted on the communication processes of the cognitive system—reading, writing, speaking, and listening. Most of these studies, however, are designed to improve the student's ability to improve these processes, as opposed to improving the mastery of knowledge itself. For example, the National Reading

Panel (2000) identified five strands that must be addressed to improve students' ability to read: vocabulary, comprehension, phonics, phonemic awareness, and frequency. Learning Bridges has in turn identified instructional strategies that make the most difference in student learning of those strands (as well as all language arts and math standards). For students from diverse cultures and children of poverty, these strategies must be modified to improve achievement and close the gaps between groups of students.

Knowledge Utilization Processes

There are four strategies that address how the brain *uses* knowledge (both declarative and procedural): *decision-making, problem-solving, investigation,* and *experimental inquiry.* Students construct personal meaning using these processing strategies. Teachers can assist them by explicitly teaching these processes using mental and graphic models to organize the information and embed it in long-term memory appropriately. In preparing to teach them, help students to set personal goals (metacognitive system). Find ways to help them to link what they already know or have experienced to the new knowledge (metacognitive system). Differentiate for your students' different learning styles by attending to the use of the visual, auditory, and kinesthetic modalities. Prepare prelearning activities using organizers such as KNLH or "before and after" to help them to record their thinking process in small groups. Teaching concept attainment, a strategy that utilizes examples and nonexamples to identify critical attributes of concepts, will prepare all students to participate in decision-making, problem-solving, inquiry, or investigation. Concept attainment allows all students to make their own personal meaning of the concepts critical to the learning tasks; the last activity in using concept attainment requires the students to verbalize how they "figured it out." Teachers can also use summarizing techniques and provide questioning stems to students to assist them in learning these processes and creating their own meaning.

We need to explicitly teach processing skills because students' past experience may have been only trial and error learning. As a result, some of them may have a tendency to give up and may lack the coping or problem-solving skills needed to resolve the barriers they encounter in learning.

These four processes are valuable at all grade levels and in all content areas; they are powerful universal processes that can be used to make meaning of any content.

When students have the opportunity to learn and apply effective problem-solving skills, they can increase achievement on learning by as much as 21 percentile points (Darling, 1999). The more relevant the problem is to the students, the more engaged they will be in the problem-solving process. For example, ask students to solve problems that involve their school day, such as finding ways to get more free time during school, finding ways to get more study time when working an after-school job, or determining how to raise money for new uniforms.

Inquiry, which requires students to generate and test hypotheses about content knowledge, can increase achievement by 37 percentile points (Darling, 1999). The beginning skills needed to conduct inquiry typically begin as whole-group activities guided by the teacher in elementary school. By middle school, teachers slowly begin to remove the scaffolding, allowing students to work through the process in small groups. If inquiry has been explored in both elementary and middle school, by high school teachers can allow students to conduct their inquiry either independently or in small groups and report their results. Refer to chapter 5, page 61, for more discussion of inquiry and investigation.

Let's look closely now at two knowledge utilization processes, *decision-making* and *problem-solving,* and see how we might teach them with our understanding of the needs of students living in poverty.

Decision-Making

Step 1: Create relevance. When introducing decision-making to your students, provide reasons why good decision-making is important in their lives. Show personal relevance to real-life experiences and provide real examples. Be sure those experiences and examples are reflective of the cultures represented in your students. Show them how to apply decision-making, as well as the difference between trivial decisions (for example, what to wear today) and complex decisions (say, choosing an elective).

Step 2: Provide examples and nonexamples. Using an advance organizer helps students to recognize the decisions they make in their daily lives, to see where and how they've made decisions in the past, to represent new alternatives, and to connect new learning to old. Have students work in cooperative groups of four when working through the organizer. In the sample in Figure 7-2, a student is deciding between the items in column 1 and column 2. Choose relevant examples for your organizer that match the situation and age of your students.

Go to school.	Take care of my little brother.
Do my homework.	Buy raffle tickets.
Make my bed.	Get a newspaper.
Pick up my clothes.	Look at a magazine.
Wash dishes.	Watch television.

Figure 7-2: A graphic organizer for a decision-making process

Step 3: Provide the steps in decision-making. Providing a visual model to your students helps them to "see" the process objectively. Ask them to do the following:

1. Identify the decision to make.

2. Write the decision question in various ways until it accurately reflects the situation.

3. Identify the choices they will consider.

4. Identify the criteria that will affect their decision.

5. Assign a score to the criteria (very important, 3; moderately important, 2; least important, 1).

There are many options for allowing students to work together on decision-making:

- Collaborative groups
- Circle sharing
- Four corners
- Group study—performance-based groups
- Partner groups
- Think, pair, share
- Cooperative learning

Figure 7-3 is an example of a matrix that uses the decision-making process to determine where to study. This is especially relevant to children of poverty, who often don't have an adequate place at home to do their schoolwork.

Next, ask students to rate the criteria and then, on a scale of zero to three, to rate the extent to which each place to study possesses the criterion.

CRITERIA	ALTERNATIVES		
	Library	Kiosk	School
Quiet			
Easy to get to			
Has computers			
Open late			

Figure 7-3: A matrix to help determine the best place to study

Next, ask them to multiply the criterion scores by the choice scores, as shown in Figure 7-4, in order to determine which choices have the highest total points.

CRITERIA	ALTERNATIVES		
	Library	Kiosk	School
Quiet (1)	3 x 1 = 3	1 x 1 = 1	2 x 1 = 2
Easy to get to (4)	2 x 2 = 4	1 x 4 = 4	3 x 4 = 12
Has computers (3)	3 x 2 = 6	1 x 3 = 3	3 x 3 = 9
Open late (2)	3 x 2 = 6	3 x 2 = 6	1 x 2 = 2

Figure 7-4: The where-to-study matrix, including choice scores multiplied by criterion scores

For a younger student, you might use these steps for a decision-making process:

- "What am I trying to decide?"

- "What are my choices?"

- "What do I want to happen, or what are some things I am looking for in a good decision?"

For a child who wants to have a pet of his or her very own: "Mom said I could have one, and I know we don't have a lot of money. Mom said if I got a pet, I will have to take care of it all by myself. How will I decide?" Use a grid like the one in Figure 7-5.

CRITERIA	ALTERNATIVES		
	Dog	Cat	Hamster
Not costly (2)	1 x 1 = 2	2 x 2 = 4	3 x 3 = 9
Easy to care for (1)	2 x 1 = 2	1 x 1 = 1	3 x 1 = 3
Do things with (3)	3 x 3 = 9	1 x 3 = 3	2 x 3 = 6
Scores	13	8	18

Figure 7-5: A decision matrix for a child choosing a pet

By using the same process that older students use, younger students can see how to weigh options in decision-making.

Sometimes, students can use this process to examine decisions they have already made that didn't work very well. Sandra tells this story from the time she was an elementary principal in a high-poverty school:

If a youngster was sent to the office for significant misbehavior on the playground or in the classroom, I would use the thinking processes to help that student to learn to make better decisions.

Typically, the student needed some quiet time to gather himself together emotionally, and I would go about my work to allow him time to compose himself. Then, I would ask what he thought had happened. You know the kind of responses I got:

"Jose hit me back first!"

"They wouldn't share the _____ with me."

"Marcus called me a name."

"I was just trying to play with them."

"I was just kidding around, and they got mad."

I would then ask him what he *did*. After a few denials and claims of innocence, with head down or looking anyplace but at me, he would finally admit what he actually did that landed him in the office.

I would ask what he *meant to happen?* What was he trying to *accomplish?*

"I wanted them to let me play with them."

"I wanted them to let me have a turn."

"I wanted them to be my friend."

"I had a better idea, and I wanted them to listen to me."

I would then ask if what he did accomplished what he *wanted*. Invariably, it did not. Then I would ask (locus of control), "Can anyone *make you* . . . [hit, swear, destroy materials, push, or whatever it was that they did]?" Sometimes he would get into the "he started it first" language, which has to be redirected back to "Who has control over your arms, legs, mouth, and so on?" conversation. Of course, he acknowledged that *he* is in charge of his arms, legs, and what he says (children of poverty often first respond with a physical reaction instead of problem-solving, remember?).

I then asked again if what he did got him what he wanted. It did not. Using prompts, I would help him make a list of other ways he could get what he wanted. We would use the decision matrix to find the best alternative together.

I then talked about *when* we could try out this new alternative. He thought of situations on the playground, classroom, and even at home where he might try this new alternative.

At this point, we moved to restitution (children of poverty often need forgiveness to restore a relationship). We would do four things:

1. I would share that a sincere apology was required and what the critical attributes of a "sincere apology" look and sound like. The student would practice delivering a sincere apology to be delivered to the teacher and the other student(s) with me serving as the practice person. This involved practicing the apology, with appropriate eye contact, body language, and voice tone, and letting the person know what he would do next time. This was his re-entry to the classroom or playground and the means for obtaining the forgiveness needed to restore the relationship that was damaged by the behavior. It also provided a lesson in how to handle a similar situation in the future.

2. The student would write a letter to the parents containing these elements:

   • A statement of what he did

   • A sincere apology

   • His plan for what he had decided was a better choice should he be faced with a similar situation

3. I would mirror positive assets to the student (efficacy building). It's important to reinforce any positive attributes of the child that he or she can bring to making very good decisions. The child is not "bad"—the *choice* was bad, and he now has a way to make a better decision and a plan to do so. Let him know that you believe that he will.

4. The student must deliver the "sincere apology" as practiced. Note: If it's not done correctly, stop the process and go back to your office and practice again. It's worth the effort! Don't assume that social skills are naturally a part of the child's repertoire. Teach them, practice them, and reinforce them. These are life skills.

I would mail the letter and keep a copy in the child's file. If the same infraction happened again, I knew the student had not been working with his plan for making better decisions. At that point, I engaged parents—not for meting out a punishment, but for finding better choices and getting support for following the plan from Mom. Interestingly, when parents of poverty realize you are not into labeling, blaming, or shaming their child or into blaming and shaming them as parents, but are truly into helping their child make better choices, their defensiveness will evaporate and they will support you in the effort. They care very much about their child!

Problem-Solving

Problem-solving is not automatically a part of the culture of many of these children, especially solutions that involve the future. They live in the moment out of necessity. As one of our principal colleagues framed it, "Could you be ready to permanently move from your living quarters in 20 minutes?" Some of our students can and do so on a regular basis. It is an "I think" and "I feel" *now* world in which these students live.

In preparation for teaching the process of problem-solving, be sure to *preteach* the vocabulary they'll need. In previous chapters, we've addressed the significance of preteaching vocabulary. Students need to know the meaning of the terms involved in the problem. In age-appropriate language, teach the vocabulary needed to understand: *goals, constraints, barriers,* and *limiting conditions.* Goals are something that students want to achieve, such as more time to pass between classes. Constraints are the forces holding one back, such as punishments for not getting to class on time. Barriers are those things that block the desired goal, such as the amount of time required of students to be in a class to get credit. Limiting conditions are those conditions that may be changed, but for now hinder solutions, such as the times that buses arrive and pick up students at school or the time that after-school sports practice begins. In order for all students to engage in the problem-solving process, they need to know the vocabulary of the process. Use the following problem steps:

1. Identify the goal (remember to attend to relevance).

2. Identify the constraints or limiting conditions (barriers).

3. If there is a constraint, identify what you are able to do without the constraint.

4. If there is a limiting condition, try to determine what you have to do to meet it and what is keeping you from doing so now.

5. Identify different ways of overcoming the constraints or meeting the limiting conditions.

6. Select and try out the alternative that appears to be the best.

7. Evaluate the effectiveness of the alternatives you have tried.

Again, remember to attend to the way you will use groups for teaching problem-solving, connect new to known, identify clearly the relevance of the issue to students' life and culture, mirror the characteristics that they already possess for engaging and learning the process, and provide a safe environment without threats for the process to unfold.

Myers-Briggs

A problem-solving process that honors the individual strengths that students bring is adapted from the Myers-Briggs Type Indicator (Myers & McCaulley, 1987). This process is very appropriate for middle school and high school students and uses cooperative groups.

1. Identify the problem to be solved and write it in a statement. Describe it in detail. What are all the facts we know? What is a realistic look at the present situation? For example, "We want more time to pass between classes, but the administration says we need so many minutes in each class." Or, "We have to have part-time jobs to pay for our clothes and entertainment, and we want to get our homework done, but we can't find the time to do both."

2. List all the possibilities that may change the situation or solve the problem, your handling of it, and other people's attitudes toward it.

3. Analyze the pros and cons of each possible solution. What are the consequences of adopting each solution? Who feels the impact of those consequences? Is there a monetary cost for any solution? Put them all in a T-chart with the pros for each solution on one side and the cons for each solution on the other. Which solution provides the most gain? Which solution is the most likely?

4. For each of the solutions, rate how deeply you care about what will be gained or lost with that solution. How will other people who are concerned about the outcome feel about the solution?

Your children of poverty will bring their personality-type strengths into different parts of the process. They can all participate in all four steps, but they will contribute the most where their strengths lie:

- Sensors are best at facing the facts and being realistic. They are the students who attend to the details of the present situation.

- Intuitors will contribute to the possibilities and to thinking outside the box. They are not so bound by "how we've always done it."

- Thinking judgers will use their impersonal analysis skills to identify cause and effect. They use logic and reasoning skills.

- Feeling judgers will make sure that values and the significance to people are heard in choosing a solution, as they seek harmony.

Teachers ask students to use each process as follows:

- By itself

- Consciously and purposefully

- In its own area of strength (for example, sensor, intuitor, thinker, feeler)

- Without interference by any other process

- In the order presented

Six Thinking Hats

Edward de Bono's *Six Thinking Hats* (1968) is another process that can be used by middle and high schools. Originally written for business and industry to add creativity and variety to problem-solving, the same process works well with students. It simplifies thinking by allowing a learner to deal with one thing at a time, in one way. The concept of the hats gives students permission to process their thinking. We often use this process in the classroom when we want students to work in small groups and add to discussions based on the hat their group has been assigned. The groups might include the following:

- **White Hat Thinkers**—Practical and rational. White Hat thinking imitates the computer, focusing only on facts and figures. Facts are evaluated in two tiers: Tier-one facts are "checked or validated facts," and tier-two facts are "unchecked but believed-to-be-true" facts. Opinions and interpretation of the facts are not permissible during White Hat thinking. (As Joe Friday of *Dragnet* fame used to say, "Just the facts.") Listening is the primary skill. However, questions focusing on the facts are permissible, as is data analysis. Choose to answer with your White Hat on. Ask the group to listen to your information with their White Hats on.

- **Yellow Hat Thinkers**—Positive assessment. Being positive is a choice. Yellow Hat thinking allows us to choose to look at things in a positive manner in order to explore how something will work. Yellow Hat thinking focuses on being constructive and making things happen. Effectiveness is the aim of Yellow Hat thinking. It focuses on possible benefits and values. Yellow Hat thinking is also used to generate proposals. It deals with soundly based optimism.

- **Gray Hat Thinkers**—Logical, critical side of thinking. This hat provides the critical judgment of why something won't work. The Gray Hat thinker points out what is wrong, incorrect, or in error. Gray Hat thinking is logical but not emotional. (Emotional negativity is Red Hat thinking). Logical and relevant reasons need to be given to support negative conclusions. The thinking must be logical and truthful, but is not always fair. (Yellow Hat thinking will balance out fairness). Gray Hat thinking is not concerned with problem-solving—only with pointing out the problem. It is best to accumulate Gray Hat thoughts as opposed to routinely throwing them out—these are barriers that need to be overcome. When considering new ideas and changes, use the Yellow Hat first and follow up with the Gray Hat.

- **Red Hat Thinkers**—Emotional, feeling, and nonrational. Red Hat thinking is the opposite of White Hat thinking. If not brought out into the open, feelings and emotions will lurk in the background and affect all thinking in a hidden way. Red Hat thinking provides a formal and defined channel for bringing these into the open. Red Hat thinking does not have to be justified. The Red Hat gives official permission for the expression of feelings that range from pure emotion to a hunch. Traditional views say that emotions mess up thinking—a good thinker is supposed to be cool and detached and not influenced by emotion. In reality, emotions influence perspective and values. Intuition is a part of Red Hat thinking. Opinions should be stated as feelings. Red Hat thinking allows an individual to say, "This is how I feel about the matter." It allows us a means to explore the feelings of others by asking for a Red Hat view. No justification or link to logic is necessary.

- **Green Hat Thinkers**—Creative thinking. Green Hat thinking involves provocation, exploration, and risk-taking. It focuses on new ideas and new ways of looking at things. It involves the deliberate creation of new ideas to develop alternatives and new approaches to problems. You cannot make yourself come up with new ideas, but you can make yourself spend time trying to develop new ideas. The Green Hat provides a formal means for doing this. The search for alternatives is a fundamental aspect of Green Hat thinking. You must go beyond the known and the obvious and the satisfactory. Green Hat thinking uses ideas as stepping stones to new ideas. Green Hat thinking also separates ideas so they can then be processed through the other thinking hats.

- **Blue Hat Thinkers**—Process control. The Blue Hat serves as a process control for the other hats, like a conductor for an orchestra. Blue Hat thinking is really thinking about thinking. You put your Blue Hat on to decide how and when to use the other hats. It defines the problems and shapes the questions. Blue Hat thinking is also responsible for summaries, overviews, and conclusions. It is used to monitor the thinking and ensures that the rules of the game are observed. Blue Hat thinking enforces the rules and stops the arguments.

Summary of Chapter Seven

When we differentiate process for children of poverty and students from diverse cultures, we must address the brain's processes at all stages of learning. All learning proceeds from the self system (volition and motivation) to the metacognitive system (goals, timelines, plans, and monitoring process) to the cognitive system (strategies for processing the information to make meaning of the content). We can and must attend to the unique needs of diverse learners in how we differentiate processes so that the gifts that our students bring to the classroom can be realized.

CHAPTER EIGHT

Differentiating Assessment

Classroom assessment can fundamentally transform the way a teacher teaches.

—W. James Popham

Participating in assessments is a part of every student's educational experience—and it is usually a very solitary one. Whether it's a spelling test or quick pop quiz, a teacher-made or textbook-prepared unit test, an essay assignment or formal presentation, an end-of-course district benchmark or a state-mandated assessment required for graduation, the traditional expectation is that students will show what they've learned independently, working alone. This expectation fits very well with the individualistic value system that dominates schools in North America. However, it poses significant problems for children from collectivist or collaborative value systems, who prefer working together. What can teachers do to help *all* students do a better job of showing what they know and are capable of doing to meet the learning expectations?

Table 8-1 provides the background we need to answer this question. It shows the types of assessments students typically encounter and how they are used.

Table 8-1: Assessment Types and Purposes and Who Benefits

Assessment	Purpose	Results
State standards, summative assessments	Analyze trend data by demographics for changes in achievement.	Inform communities, state departments, district administrators, principals, teachers, parents, and students on how students compare with others within a state on learning expectations (that is, state standards).
	Fulfill federal reporting requirement for No Child Left Behind.	Typically used to identify schools and districts not making adequate yearly progress (AYP), with its accompanying sanctions; sometimes used for school improvement planning and program evaluation
State benchmarks, formative assessments	Analyze student achievement by state benchmarks during the school year.	Inform district administrators, principals, teachers, parents, and students on what students have learned and what they still need to learn for the school year's learning expectations to drive decisions on curriculum pacing, instruction, and interventions needed.
		Sometimes used for school improvement planning
District summative assessments (end-of-grade or course; criterion-referenced district assessments)	Analyze student achievement of district curriculum.	Inform district administrators, principals, teachers, parents, and students on what students have learned in a particular grade or course based on the district's curriculum.
		Used for grading and curriculum evaluation
Classroom formative assessments created by teachers	Analyze learning of specific objectives within a unit of instruction for mastery.	Inform teachers, parents, and students on what has been learned well enough and when an additional opportunity to learn must be provided (reteaching) because adequate mastery has not been achieved.
		Also informs grading
Classroom formative assessments produced by curriculum products (that is, textbooks)	Analyze learning of specific objectives taught in the curriculum materials for mastery.	Inform teachers, parents, and students on what has been learned from curriculum materials and when reteaching or interventions need to occur.
		May also inform grading

As you can see from the table, the primary distinction between assessments is formative versus summative. Chappuis & Chappuis (2007/2008) describe formative assessment as "an ongoing, dynamic process that involves far more than frequent testing" (p. 15). It provides information to both teachers and students during the instructional assessment. Summative testing, on the other hand, is usually used to a) make some kind of judgment about the learning, b) to determine if a student is to be passed on to the next grade, c) to measure adequate yearly progress, or d) to measure the effectiveness of a program being delivered in the school.

Teachers sometimes feel that, whatever type of assessment they are using, they are assessing their students way too much. Many complain that assessment is taking too much time away from instruction (Ohanian, 2001; Popham, 2002). And sometimes they are right! Especially since the passage of No Child Left Behind, classroom and formal testing have increased (Stiggins, 1997), and many assessments are mandated for purposes that don't have very much impact on teaching and learning.

Our focus here is on those assessments that *do* make a difference both in instruction and student performance—and over which we have some control. In this chapter, we will look at how assessment affects learning and then examine how we can differentiate assessments in order to better measure learning for children of poverty and diverse cultures. We will also address how we can better prepare our students for high-stakes tests that are mandated.

When Assessments Make a Difference

Here are some rules of thumb to measure the power of an assessment to make a difference in learning for students:

1. The more the assessment is about checking for understanding of what is explicitly taught in the classroom, the more the results can be used to inform teachers and students about both teaching and learning.

2. The sooner the assessment is given following the learning, the more likely it is to measure what has been learned, particularly if it is designed to reflect how the curriculum was taught in the classroom (that is, if the language of instruction matches the language of assessment).

3. The tighter the alignment between the curriculum (what we say we want students to learn), the instruction (how teachers provide relevant, culturally responsive opportunities to learn), and assessment (how we measure whether learning has occurred), the more likely the results will reflect what has actually been learned.

4. The more the assessment is appropriately designed for the type of knowledge (declarative or procedural) that it measures, the more likely the results are to measure that knowledge.

5. The more that assessment is used as a learning tool, the more students will pay attention to the results.

6. The more students are engaged in how they will demonstrate their learning and the more they know ahead of time about how it will be measured, the more they will attend to the results of the assessment.

Checking for Understanding of What's Been Taught

Tomlinson (2007, 2008), when discussing principles of assessment, reminds us that "informative assessment isn't just about tests" (p. 10). Students can demonstrate what they've learned through observation, discussions in which rich ideas are generated, solving problems they are presented with, drawing illustrations, role-playing, and in a variety of other ways. When used as a check for understanding, assessment is not separate from curriculum and instruction but informs teachers how curriculum and instruction must be adjusted to meet students' learning needs. Such assessment is therefore continuous and ongoing. Students can also use this kind of assessment, particularly if it comes in the form of self-assessment as a check for understanding.

Let's look at the ways teachers differentiate assessment in classrooms that serve students living in poverty and students of color.

A High School Literature Assessment

Four students (three Latino and one African American student) are seated together, with their desks clustered, in a high school English class. For materials, they have the following:

- Four copies of *The Diary of Anne Frank,* the story they are to read and analyze

- Four copies of the assignment, which consists of "responses to the literature"—relating it to their personal lives, describing ways it could be presented (music, dance, written essay, multimedia, art, and so on), and tasks for the group to accomplish

- Four copies of the assessment rubric, which describes the criteria for success on the written assignment and the levels of performance

Students discuss whether to read the book together or independently. One student remarks that he isn't a great reader and would prefer they read it together aloud. Another comments that if they are going to do that, they will have to do it before school, because she works at a fast-food restaurant after school. The students make decisions together about how to approach the task of reading and discuss how they will respond to the literature, what the items of the assessment rubric mean, and what questions they want to ask the teacher to clarify the rubric items. Each student is responsible for part of what is required. The students will work together while learning and decide together how they will demonstrate what they know and are able to do in a way that fits their interests and cultural value systems, while meeting the criteria of the rubric. There are no "gotchas" for these students, because they know up front what constitutes an excellent response, and they have options to demonstrate their learning. Andrade (2007, 2008) speaks to the power of rubrics to self-assess and to open the door for feedback, which we know has a powerful impact on student learning.

Choral Response to Questioning at a Middle School

The teacher in this math lesson is checking for understanding of the meaning of the vocabulary of the measurement unit. Students are seated at round tables instead of desks. Materials—located in the center of the table in community containers—include crayons, markers, rulers, scissors, and so on. Student groups have collaboratively created attribute wheels for the new vocabulary words on a single sheet of backing paper. The teacher walks around during the construction of the wheels, answering any questions, redirecting the thinking in the small groups, and reinforcing the students' collaborative efforts. The teacher then stands in front of the classroom and asks questions about the vocabulary word meanings, and the students respond as a group. They are readily able to participate because of the attribute wheels, the collaborative process used to define the words, and the collaborative means of assessing for understanding. Again, this means of assessment meets the needs of students from collectivist, or group, value systems.

Buddy Support at an Elementary School

Children in an extremely high-poverty elementary classroom are getting ready for a practice test on their benchmark assessment. They each have an assigned "study buddy" in this classroom. The process used by this teacher is described by Rothstein-Fisch, Trumbull, Isaac, Daley, and Perez (2003, pp. 132–134). Each pair of children has been studying the sample questions together on a practice test booklet, determining what the question is asking, identifying the answer that is for sure wrong, and reasoning together regarding what they will choose for an answer. When the buddies decide they're ready, they *both* go up to their teacher. The teacher asks the questions they studied together, while the buddy stands by quietly supporting his fellow student. When the participating student demonstrates mastery by correctly answering the questions, the buddy rings a bell and announces to the rest of the class that his or her study buddy is now ready to pass the formative or benchmark assessment. The entire class cheers their group member, who has just prepared and passed the practice test with collaborative preparation. The two students then switch places, and the other child is assessed. This process "did not single out the student being tested, but rather highlighted the team that worked together for the benefit of the whole group. Without any disruption, the students clapped and immediately returned to their work" (Rothstein-Fisch & Trumbull, 2008, p. 149).

This is collaborative preparation and individual accountability for learning. The sooner the assessment occurs following explicit instruction, the more successful the student and the more relevant the results will be to modifying instruction and providing feedback to the student as to what he or she knows and still needs to learn.

Cooperative Learning Groups: Practicing for Formative Assessment

Describing a Bridging Cultures Project classroom, Rothstein-Fisch and Trumbull (2008) identify another way to prepare for formative and summative assessments using practice tests that meet the needs of students from collectivist or group cultures. These practice tests use a multiple-choice format. They may or may not use the language of instruction in the assessment items. The teacher knows that the students are required to take the benchmark or formative assessments independently, which may cause stress for students from a collectivist culture. To differentiate the test preparation process to meet the needs of many of the students in the class living in poverty and many of the students of color, the teacher uses a three-part process:

1. Students take the practice test *individually.*

2. Students, in cooperative groups, *collaboratively* correct the practice test.

3. The entire class *collaboratively* analyzes the correct and incorrect responses.

This process recognizes the need for individual assessment and provides students with practice taking them. However, the collaborative correcting of the practice test also allows students to together identify differences between the language of instruction and the language of assessment—and to help one another to understand. This collaborative analysis of correct and incorrect responses has a number of benefits: Students are prepared to take their benchmark formative assessments independently; they are more comfortable demonstrating what they have learned; and there is both individual accountability in the individual assessment and group success in the cooperative learning that preceded it.

Aligned Assessment

"We didn't learn about that!"

"That wasn't in the book."

"I think I studied the wrong things."

"Half the stuff on this test covered material that the teacher never talked about in class. That's unfair!"

These are comments from students complaining about assessments they've suffered through. Is there any possibility that their complaints are justified?

We believe most students from elementary school through college have experienced assessment that is disconnected from both curriculum (learning expectations) and instruction (the experiences provided by teachers for students to learn the curriculum). If assessments are not testing what was stated as the learning expectations and what was taught by their teachers, *then* the results are not going to measure either the curriculum or the learning. Students perceive such assessments as unfair, as "gotchas," and so it doesn't matter if they pay attention and participate in class. It doesn't matter if they study what was taught, nor is it helpful for them to focus on what was stated as the learning expectations, because the key processes in education—namely, curriculum, instruction, and assessment—are not aligned. The test isn't going to measure their efforts.

Triangulating for Alignment

What can classroom teachers do about alignment? Teachers can "triangulate" or check for alignment of the following:

1. The stated learning *expectations* (standards, curriculum, and objectives); what we say we want students to learn

2. The *instruction* (activities, experiences, listening, and so on) that provide students with the means to learn the stated learning expectations—instructional strategies for teachers and learning activities, assignments, and products for students

3. The *assessment* items or tasks that specifically measure learning of the standards, curriculum, or objectives and reflect the language of instruction, not some other format

When triangulating expectation, instruction, and assessment, it is important to determine how many items are in the assessment for each objective. It is also important that the assessment reflect the amount of time spent in instruction. In other words, the number of items for a particular learning objective should be appropriate to the time spent teaching to that objective. A well-aligned assessment does not have a large number of items on a learning expectation that is a) unimportant to the larger standards and goals expected to be learned, or b) insignificant based on the amount of time spent by educators teaching it and the time on task provided for students to learn it.

Triangulation Checklist: Mr. Jenkins' Class

Mr. Jenkins has identified specific learning expectations for a unit of study; he has also identified activities, assignments, and learning experiences that he will provide his students during his teaching of the unit; and he has created an assessment that he feels will measure the student learning that has occurred. Now he wants to "triangulate" his planning efforts to assure alignment. He uses the following checklist to assist him:

1. Does the unit contain *clear outcomes,* appropriate for the student audience, that describe the learning expectation? (expectation)

2. Are these outcomes drawn from specific *state standards?* (expectation)

3. Are the *instructional strategies* that were chosen effective for the concepts and processes stated in the learning expectations? (learning)

4. Will the student activities, assignments, and learning experiences that provide the *opportunity to learn* the outcomes provide *adequate time and practice* with available options for differentiation? (learning)

5. Are *all* of the outcomes adequately addressed in the activities, assignments, and learning experiences, with none left out? (learning)

6. Are *all* of the outcomes, or learning expectations, assessed appropriately? (assessment)

7. Is the *means of assessment* (for example, multiple choice, essay, rubrics, performance tasks, and so on) appropriate for assessing both kinds of knowledge with options for differentiation? (assessment)

8. Is the *language of assessment* the same as that used in instruction? (assessment)

9. Is the *number of items or tasks* appropriate for the significance of the content and processes being measured, as well as the length of time spent in teaching and learning them? (assessment)

Mrs. Coleman's Class: Team Planning That Requires Aligning

The students in Mrs. Coleman's class are about to begin a new unit of instruction. As a part of her introduction, she places students in groups of four and gives them an outline of the activities, assignments, and tasks that they will be engaged in, complete with quality indicators for performance and the ways in which they will be assessed. The students design a group learning plan using the teacher's outline, shown in Table 8-2.

Table 8-2: Group Learning Plan Created by Mrs. Coleman's Students

Learner Outcome(s)	Assignments, Activities, and Tasks to Be Accomplished	How and Where Assessed
Demonstrate understanding of the foundational documents, including the Constitution and the Bill of Rights.	Read each document, and as a group, compare and contrast citizen rights and responsibilities assigned in each document. Prepare a visual representation demonstrating the rights and responsibilities of these two documents. Identify the critical attributes of key terminology and concepts used in the documents with attribute wheels.	Team Evaluation Checklist that contains the quality indicators for the visual representations as a result of the compare/contrast process Attribute Wheels for the key terminology and concepts identified from the Constitution and Bill of Rights Quiz on terminology and concept meanings in each document
Identify persisting issues involving rights, roles, and status of individuals in relation to the general welfare of society.	Participate in jurisprudential inquiry in small groups, with a review of a case study on gay marriage, immigration, the Patriot Act, affirmative action, or another issue approved by the teacher, but submitted by the team.	Group presentation of findings, including a clear identification of the issues, the perspectives presented, and an identification of the conclusions reached and the rationale for each; class and instructor evaluation rubrics filled out for the team that contain quality performance indicators
Demonstrate understanding of how citizens can affect public policy.	Read and research in cooperative groups the ways in which citizens, noncitizens, and dual citizens can have an impact on public policy in an area of interest approved by the teacher—for example, immigration, environment, education, labor, gun registration, and so on. Write an expository paper to be shared with the class.	Rubric that contains quality indicators for both the writing process and the content to be addressed Evaluation checklists for the oral presentation to be used by both the class and the teacher; checklists to be compiled by the team for self-assignment of a grade

At this point, student groups begin to identify timelines, assign roles and tasks among themselves, lay out the sequence of the tasks, and begin the processes of learning. It is easier to see the connections between the outcomes, student learning experiences and tasks, and assessment when *the students themselves* have laid it out this way to begin their team planning. If the alignment is not readily understood, they will find it.

Assessing for Type of Knowledge

There are many ways that teachers assess students to measure outcomes or the expectations of learning. Gwen Doty (2007) in the Learning Bridges class entitled "Classroom Assessment and Data Analysis," does an excellent job of helping us to understand the significance of choosing appropriate assessments for different types of knowledge. All learning expectations, whether for the curriculum that we teach or the state standards to which the curriculum is aligned, represent two types of knowledge: *declarative* and *procedural*. Declarative knowledge consists of information. That information could be terminology, facts, or concepts. Procedural knowledge consists of the skills and processes that are performed with the information. Those skills and processes could include algorithms, comparing, analyzing, synthesizing, categorizing, problem-solving, and so on. Each type of knowledge, as Doty explains, requires its own appropriate assessment.

We also need to remember that scores and test results on any single assessment should be considered collected data to help you, the teacher, to make judgments about a student's performance on the content you are teaching. Think back to a time when you did poorly on a huge test for whatever reason, yet you were sure that you really *knew* the information! It's unfair to our students to assess only through a final test. We should be assessing throughout the learning process. This could take place through observations, anecdotal notes, student learning journals, daily assignments, oral discussions, and so on. Of course you will also want to have a culminating final assessment that would probably carry more weight.

Let's examine some assessment types and see what type of knowledge—declarative or procedural—each is best used for.

- *Criterion-referenced* assessments refers to tests that measure achievement based on a predetermined standard or set of criteria. Criterion-referenced tests may originate from the district or from a textbook, or they could be written by the teacher. They are usually created as selected-response tests and often scored on a percentage basis *(declarative)*.

- *Standardized or norm-referenced tests* are also usually created with a selected-response format. What sets this assessment apart from criterion-referenced assessments is that the results are compared to a norm group of test takers rather than to a standard or predetermined criteria *(declarative)*.

- *Standards-based assessments* include any assessment that is based on the predetermined *taught* standards or criteria that are aligned with what is tested (assessment). Student scores are compared to the predetermined goals or criteria rather than to other student scores. The term standards-based assessments is very broad and includes any of the following formats: portfolios, performances, projects, essays, or presentations *(declarative or procedural)*.

- *Performance assessments* involve students' oral or written presentations. An effective performance assessment would be a standards-based assessment that is scored with a rubric *(declarative or procedural)*.

- *Portfolio assessments* are very appropriate for classroom use, as teachers can use them to see samplings of various genres and the progression of student improvement over a long period of time. Portfolios could also be considered to be performance assessments. If portfolios are aligned to the standards taught and tested, then they may also be considered standards-based assessments. For example, a new teacher, Dawne Harwood, labeled accordion files that she kept in a file crate for each student. Although as a sixth-grade teacher, she taught all subject areas, she decided to use portfolios only for language arts and chose eight language arts standards to assess through portfolio assessment. She then created a rubric for each of those eight standards.

Throughout the school year, Ms. Harwood collected first- and final-draft writing samples for each of the eight standards taught. With each of these student submissions, she asked students to complete a reflections entry to describe their planning stages for each piece, their feelings about the writing project in general, and their feelings about each final piece. In May, she was able to compare student writing abilities from the beginning to the end of the year. She was also able to determine consistent strengths and weaknesses during the year by comparing various genres of writing. And perhaps most importantly, she was able to review the reflection entries written by students throughout the year to determine their confidence levels and attitudes about the writing process. This helped her to provide specific feedback to each student about their writing. Throughout the year, Ms. Harwood was also able to see the progress of her ELL students' writing and determine in which areas she could best foster their written language *(declarative or procedural).*

- *Formative assessment,* as we have seen, is another very broad term encompassing many formats in which students are actively involved and are presented with opportunities to reflect on the learning. Formative assessment could be considered a diagnostic tool to provide feedback to students over the course of instruction *(declarative or procedural).*

- *Authentic or natural assessment* develops naturally from instruction, rather than the other way around. It involves students in real life situations and projects from which the standards can be learned. For example, after a second-grade class learns the standards of adding and subtracting with money, they set up a snack bar during a school baseball game. Students are in charge of all of the addition and subtraction of funds in the snack bar. They are assessed through an observation check sheet that the teacher has created. This type of assessment can be extremely valuable, in that students will be engaged in the learning and highly motivated. The downside is that it can be extremely time-consuming both in the planning stage and during the lesson itself *(declarative or procedural)*.

- *Selected-response assessments* are the typical tests to which most of us have become accustomed. They include formats such as true/false, multiple choice, matching, and fill in the blank. Most criterion-referenced and standardized tests use a selected-response format. These tests certainly have their place in the classroom setting, but teachers must keep in mind the varying intelligence strengths and weaknesses of their students when using them. You may, for example, have a student with high visual and kinesthetic intelligences who does poorly on this type of test but excels when given opportunities to create graphic representations, projects, and presentations. In addition, English-language learners may not be able to read the selected-response test questions and may perform poorly even if they truly do understand the taught concepts *(declarative)*.

Table 8-3 (page 156) summarizes which assessments to use in a given situation.

Table 8-3: Choosing the Appropriate Assessment

Assessment	Format	Example	Best Used
Criterion-referenced test	Individual measurement of skills or objectives often measured with a percentage; usually composed of selected-response items	Teacher-made test; district assessment tests.	With declarative knowledge; subject specific; when needing to score quickly
Standardized or norm-referenced test	Compares all test-takers to each other and is measured with a curve to demonstrate level of proficiency; usually composed of selected-response items	Stanford 9 Achievement Test	With declarative knowledge; subject specific; often sent out of school to be scanned and scored electronically
Standards-based assessment	Often less structured; compares individuals with predetermined objectives, takes into account alignment of curriculum, instruction, and assessment; usually assessed with a rubric	An essay, poem, group problem-solving project that stemmed from aligned curriculum and instruction; rubric reflects the taught standards	With declarative or procedural knowledge; thinking and reasoning skills
Performance assessment	General term for all assessments that require the learner to create, produce, perform, design, construct, invent, etc. a final product; usually assessed through a rubric	Formal presentation, skit, project, science experiment display, and so on	With declarative or procedural knowledge; thinking and reasoning standards
Portfolio assessment	A type of performance assessment that represents a sampling of a particular student's achievement or progress; usually assessed through a rubric	An accordion file where language arts students submit selected pieces from the various genres that are studied	With declarative or procedural knowledge; thinking and reasoning standards
Formative assessment	General term for ongoing assessment used to inform teachers regarding instruction and students regarding their learning in progress; accumulates over time	Journal entries, lab reports, portfolio submissions	With declarative or procedural knowledge; thinking and reasoning standards
Summative assessment	A type of assessment (usually a structured format) used at the end of a semester, quarter, unit, or end of course	Unit test in textbook	With declarative knowledge; subject specific; when needing to score quickly
Authentic or natural assessment	A term that implies real-world or meaningful assessment that is incorporated as a part of the learning process	Buying groceries, totaling the cost, and finding the average price for selected items	With declarative or procedural knowledge; thinking and reasoning standards
Selected-response assessment	Format in which students select a right or wrong answer	True/false, multiple choice, matching	With declarative knowledge; subject specific; when needing to score quickly

Rothstein-Fisch & Trumbull (2008) urge teachers to provide as many opportunities as possible when assessing for students to work together to meet the needs of children of poverty and students from diverse cultures. Some of the assessments shown in the table are conducive to collaboration; others must be independently done. However, even those tests that are completed independently can be practiced for in groups. For example, student groups can analyze questions on practice tests, determine how to find the easiest options to discard, and figure out how to provide a rationale for the correct response as part of the learning process. The collaborative work and success with formative assessments can predict success with individually completed, summative assessments where an "evaluation" on learning is done, such as in state standards tests.

Assessment as a Learning Tool: Mrs. Cabral's Classroom

If you were to step inside Mrs. Cabral's first/second-grade classroom in Sacramento, you would see 6- and 7-year-old children eager to see their assessment results. Mrs. Cabral's classroom is in an area of extreme poverty, with a very high percentage of her students new to this country and from different cultures. You would hear them asking when the next test would be given so they could show what they've learned. "Can we do it again tomorrow?" Why are they so eager to be assessed?

Like all of the other teachers in her school, Mrs. Cabral administers formative assessments assigned by the district. But she approaches assessment with these children not as a tool to label or sort them, but as something from which both she and they can learn.

Identifying the Misconceptions

Before every lesson, Mrs. Cabral lets her children know what they are going to be learning *and* how she and they will know it. The culture in her classroom reflects her assumption that all students are expected to learn the knowledge or skill being taught. This culture allows for students to help each other in the learning process. It also provides an opportunity for them to prepare for the assessments together *before* that assessment is individually administered. Mrs. Cabral meets with the children in small groups to analyze the language of the questions. They also analyze the format of the answers. The content to be measured is analyzed as students cheer each other on when they give correct responses and share their "a-ha" moments as they identify misconceptions. Mrs. Cabral praises them for these insights, and the group does a quick compare and contrast between the misconception and the more accurate response to identify why the misunderstandings occurred. This is learning in progress. The children now perceive themselves as learners and tell Mrs. Cabral, "Let me try again! I've got it now!"

Error Analysis

Mrs. Cabral's students have learned from her that she expects every single one of them to achieve proficiency on the test. There are several options: She will work with them one-on-one, they can help one another, or they can work in groups. The high expectation is that everyone in her class can be proficient. After the test, she shares the results with the class as a whole. With simple graphical representations, they view their results as a class—without knowing the names of individual students. Proficiency is framed in terms of the class as a whole, not as an individual goal. There are bars on the graph for every learner outcome. The marks on the left side indicate levels of proficiency, enabling the class to see what they know and what they still need to learn. They examine together the areas where the class is scoring low. They look at each question to see what it is asking and how it was like or unlike their classroom experiences while learning, and then Mrs. Cabral goes over the answer and the errors. She does not identify who made the error at that time. No student is singled out, labeled, or shamed. Instead, the entire class analyzes the errors to see if there is an a-ha moment for them. You can watch the understanding happen in their faces. They are learning—using assessment as the vehicle. Yes, some students are going to need one-on-one attention, and yes, it's hard for her to find the time. Sometimes she acknowledges that she didn't teach something very well and that she'll teach it again. (Note her assumption of responsibility: It isn't that they didn't learn well enough; *she* didn't *teach* well enough.) However, these students are consistently meeting their expectations in both math and reading assessments, and they often exceed them. Mrs. Cabral's students achieve the *proficient* label over and over again . . . individually and collaboratively as a class. It is heartening to hear the cheers on the next try!

Student Choice and Voice in Assessment

It is often difficult to provide very young students with choices in how they will learn and a voice in how they will be assessed. However, by the middle of elementary school, students are usually able to participate in choosing options both in how they best learn and how they best can show what they've learned. For example, students can have an option to demonstrate their learning through a written report, the creation of a skit or rap, an oral presentation, or some other form.

Multiple Intelligences

Gardner's work (1999) on multiple intelligences is an extremely useful tool for teachers for differentiating, or providing choices, in the area of how a student will learn. It can also be used to differentiate assessment. A Google search for "multiple intelligences assessment" turned up nearly half a million results.

Our students bring different intelligences to the classroom, for learning as well as for assessing that learning. And the way students learn best is also the way they want to be assessed. If a student is a strong verbal linguistic learner, he or she may be most comfortable showing what has been learned through the use of words—either verbally or in written form. Students who have strong mathematical-logical skills might want choices that engage their problem-solving skills or their ability to discern numerical and logical patterns. Allowing them to show what they know through cause and effect, the use of logic, or finding patterns and relationships will better showcase what they've learned.

Schools typically recognize and reward both these types of intelligence. However, students also need an opportunity to learn, and to demonstrate that they've learned, through music and rhythm and through art and the relationships of objects in space. If they are strong in bodily-kinesthetic intelligence, they need an opportunity to use movement and performance. Students who have strong *inter*personal skills learn and show their learning best when relating, communicating, and working with others. Students with strong *intra*personal intelligence may need to be allowed ways to show the results of their reflections, understandings, and thinking processes in their assessments.

Like all other students, our students living in poverty and from diverse cultures have their preferences. When we allow them to have choices based on their strengths and a voice in how they will be assessed, they will increase the effort they put into the learning and attend to the results more seriously.

Individual vs. Collaborative Work

Some of us learn best alone; others learn best together. Some students do well with individual assessments; others can better show what they've learned in a collaborative effort. Another way to provide student choices in learning and assessing is by giving them a choice about whether to work independently or collaboratively. There is a place for both. Of course, teachers do not always get to choose how assessments are given, but the *preparation* for those individually administered assessments is usually within the control of the teacher. By providing choices to students whenever we can in how they will be assessed, we will increase their learning and, consequently, the results of assessment.

Summary of Chapter Eight

In summary, as teachers, we have opportunities to differentiate assessment experiences for our students so that all of them can demonstrate the knowledge and skills they have acquired in the teaching and learning process. We can provide opportunities for all of our students, including those from diverse cultures and those living in poverty, to respond eagerly to assessment. We want all of our students to ask, "I've got it now; when can I try again?"

CHAPTER NINE

Bringing It Together to Build Resilience in Diverse Students

A common finding in resilience research is the power of a teacher—often without realizing it—to tip the scale from risk to resilience. . . . The bottom line and starting point for creating turnaround classrooms and schools that provide caring relationships, high expectations, and opportunities for participation is the deep belief on the part of teachers and school staff that every child and youth has innate resilience, the capacity for healthy development and successful learning.

—Bonnie Benard

In previous chapters, we have examined the relationship of culture and poverty to the learning needs of children and youth. The needs of children of extreme poverty resonate personally with both of us. Why did *we* overcome the obstacles inherent in poverty? Both of us had teachers who believed in us (and some teachers who didn't!). But because of the ones who did, and the resilience we developed in their classrooms, we hoped and believed that we could do whatever was put before us. We believe that you can choose to be one of those turnaround teachers for the children of poverty and from diverse cultures in your classroom.

Fostering Resilience

Resilient children succeed academically and socially despite the severe situations and obstacles they face. We cannot wave a magic wand to make the obstacles inherent in poverty disappear. But we *can* foster in our students the resilience to succeed academically in spite of those obstacles.

Henderson & Milstein (1996) developed a model that suggests that resilience is made up of twelve factors internal to the child:

1. A good, strong sense of selflessness, or giving of one's self

2. The possessing of life skills, such as good decision-making, self-control, and assertiveness

3. An ability to be sociable

4. A sense of humor

5. An internal locus of control

6. Autonomy

7. Orientation toward a positive future

8. Adaptability and flexibility

9. An interest in and connection to learning

10. Self-motivation

11. Personal competence in one or multiple areas

12. Some element of self-worth or self-efficacy

As teachers, we can assist in fostering resilience by establishing nurturing, culturally responsive environments for our diverse students, rather than focusing on programs that concentrate on their academic deficits. In fact, a common finding in resilience research is the quality of the teacher's input. Benard (2003) talks about the practices of "turnaround teachers," teachers who build resilient students in the face of overwhelming odds. These teachers establish caring relationships, hold high expectations for *every* student, and provide opportunities for student participation and contribution for all children. Benard states, "These three protective factors are so powerful because they are how students—and everyone else—meet the basic human needs for love and belonging; for respect, power, accomplishment, and learning; and ultimately for meaning" (2003, p. 125).

She further suggests that we identify the most challenging student we have in our classroom. Look for and identify all of that student's strengths and mirror them back to the student. Teach him or her that they have innate resilience and the power to create their own reality. Create opportunities to have the student participate and contribute his or her strengths. Be patient and focus on small victories, which often grow into major transformations. We can do this!

Waxman, Gray, and Padron (2003) in their *Review of Research on Education Resilience,* focused research studies on Latino and African American students who were poor and successful in school, and those who were not. As a result, they identified what they termed *educational resilience.* The research on building educational resilience in diverse learners suggests that teachers can create the conditions to assure academic achievement and close the achievement gaps through (1) culturally responsive classroom environments (*context*), (2) attending to the processes by which students make meaning through instruction (*process*), and (3) contextualizing the *content* and modifying the *products* so students can demonstrate their learning.

McMillan and Reed (1994) address four factors that impact on differentiating context and process (chapters 5 and 7) to build educational resilience:

- Personal attributes like motivation and goal orientation; the self and metacognitive systems (*process*)

- Positive use of time (for example, on-task behavior, homework completion, participation in extracurricular experiences) where students need assistance; metacognitive system (*process*)

- Family life (family support and expectations) where teachers can meet the needs of a collectivist value system (*context)*

- School and classroom learning environment that is culturally responsive to diverse children of poverty (*context*)

Gonzalez and Padilla (1997) examined poor Mexican American high school students to identify contributing factors to resilience. As with the McMillan and Reed study before it, they found that Latino children of poverty had significantly higher perceptions of family and peer support and a greater sense of belonging in their cultural group and family than nonresilient students. Alva (1991) worked with 10th-grade Mexican American children of poverty who were resilient and who maintained a high grade-point average. When she interviewed them, they reported that they felt they were prepared to attend college, liked coming to school, and had fewer conflicts and difficulties with other Mexican American students or with their families. Waxman and Huang (1996), Waxman, Padron, and Arnold (2001), Henderson and Milstein (1996), and Benard (1997) all substantiate this:

- Differentiating the instructional context experiences for diverse students to meet their cultural needs in order creates the right environmental conditions in the classroom.

- Attending to the processes of instruction to meet the needs for interaction, relationship-building, efficacy, motivation, organizational skills, time management, and relevancy builds more resilience in students.

- Holding high expectations, creating personal relationships, and providing opportunities to learn and participate collaboratively when addressing the learning tasks (for example, content) and products created, fosters resilience.

As we reviewed the literature and research on what teachers might do to meet the needs of diverse learners so they can achieve, we discovered over and over that we need to differentiate context, content and products, and process to meet the unique needs of these students. We also discovered that when we do differentiate instruction in this way, we build resilience in our diverse learners so they can succeed academically.

We believe we can both improve academic achievement *and* close the achievement gaps with a research-based differentiation model for children of poverty and diverse cultures. In doing so, we address the variables that we have control over and can implement in school to build the resilience in our students to succeed. This is shown graphically in Figure 9-1.

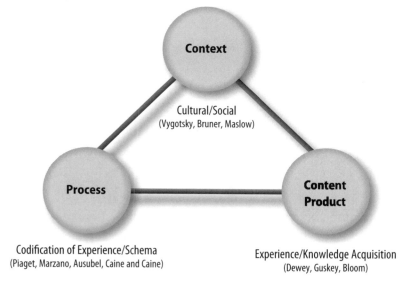

Figure 9-1: A model of teaching and learning connections, derived from Williams, 2003, p. 23

Grounded in research, this theoretical model provides for the needs of African Americans, Native Americans, Hispanic Americans, urban and rural populations, and children of poverty. We believe this model can also be applied to other cultures, even though the data is sparse.

How to Use the Two Rubrics

To provide you with a way to find what you want quickly, we have developed two rubrics (Tables 9-1 and 9-2) for your use in determining where to begin to differentiate instruction.

Instructional Needs Rubric

Use this model when you encounter instructional difficulties. You may have provided very clear directions for a complex task. They are written out for students in a handout. But your students still don't seem to know where to begin . . . so they don't begin. Your instructional difficulty challenge appears to be to provide them with a way to plan, organize, and manage time to accomplish this task. This first rubric will help you quickly identify ways to address the instructional difficulty through context, content and product, and process with highly effective instructional strategies.

Differentiation Steps Rubric

You have identified a specific unit of instruction that you want to teach. You know the learning expectations for that unit based on your grade level standards. You want to differentiate some of the lessons within the unit for your diverse students. To effectively plan how to do that, you can work through the steps of the differentiation model and quickly identify highly effective ways to ensure that your students achieve. The second rubric will help you to do that. (Step 1, if you remember, is building teacher background knowledge. We did not include that in the rubric, but this critical piece is where teachers need to begin (see chapter 3, page 31). Acquiring our own background knowledge allows the shift in our "set of glasses," so that we can successfully differentiate instruction for our diverse students.

When you design classroom practices that meet the specific needs your children of poverty bring, you are fostering the resilience in those students to succeed. By providing the environment, the caring, the high expectations, and the effective instructional practices that can override poverty, you will create resilient, confident, competent learners who believe they *can,* and who actually *do it!*

In closing, we believe that you, the reader, now have an excellent understanding of how to modify your teaching practice to override the impact of poverty and lift your students to a new level of performance.

Summary of *Why Culture Counts*

We promised a model that would provide you with the knowledge and skills to do the following:

- Build resilience in children of poverty and students from diverse cultures, and children new to North America.

- Create relevancy for students of diverse cultures.

- Increase a student's sense of efficacy and confidence both as a person and a learner.

- Build the background knowledge necessary to level the learning playing field.

- Activate prior knowledge and experiences in order to address a new learning task as well as to facilitate storage and retrieval of information through more than the semantic pathway to the brain.

- Recognize and respect relationships and social knowledge that are critical to continued success.

- Create the brain-compatible conditions and hold the high expectations that allow for the success of every child as he or she engages in the learning tasks of schools.

- Differentiate: (a) context, (b) content and product, and (c) process to assure successful engagement of diverse learners and students living in poverty.

We will leave you with a quote from Al Mamary, the former superintendent of Johnson City Schools in New York: "Given what we *know* about education, it is unethical and morally wrong not to *act* on that knowledge." We concur.

Table 9-1: Instructional Needs Rubric

Instructional Need	Differentiating Context in a Culturally Responsive Classroom	Differentiating Process for Systems of Thinking (Self, Metacognitive, Cognitive)	Differentiating Content and Product	Research-Based Instructional Strategies
To allow for the significance of relationships	Build on student interests and collectivist values.	Self system—Provide a variety of ways in which students can learn together and strengthen acceptance of differences (through collaborative groups, circle sharing, four corners, group study, partner groups, think, pair, share, cooperative learning, peer evaluations, and so on).	Provide the scaffolding for success.	Create a learning state that has moderate difficulty, high feedback, and low tension.
	Incorporate student background culture.		Provide consistency.	Cooperative learning +28 percentile points
	Choose classroom and materials that reflect the cultural diversity of the classroom.		Eliminate "gotchas."	Use feedback and encouragement.
	Emphasize quality learning for everyone.		Give students choices.	Tell students up front the personal importance of the lesson (how this will help them meet a personal goal or fill a personal need).
	Understand the basis of relationships in the culture you are teaching.		Provide a rubric and consistently grade according to that rubric.	

(Continued)

Instructional Need	Differentiating Context in a Culturally Responsive Classroom	Differentiating Process for Systems of Thinking (Self, Metacognitive, Cognitive)	Differentiating Content and Product	Research-Based Instructional Strategies
To increase self efficacy, particularly as a learner	Teach to student modalities. Mirror back strengths to students. Use affirmations. Honor culture of family and community by contextualizing curriculum and instruction. Value all types of intelligences. Use the abundance model and help students build on their gifts. Provide opportunities to contribute and participate.	Self system—Build beliefs students can achieve as learners based on assets. Metacognitive system—Strengthen students' ability to set goals and monitor how they are doing with the strategies they've selected to attain the goals.	Start with kids where they are and move them up Bloom's Taxonomy. Provide choices. Let students choose to work above level but never below their abilities.	Explicit feedback +37 percentile points Praise with successively more difficult attempts +27 percentile points Praise—Effort +29 percentile points Wait time +40 percentile points Disposition and process monitoring +33 percentile points
To teach planning, organization, and time-management skills	Tap into prior learning and experience based on the cultures represented in the classroom. Tie prior learning and experiences to the new learning. Explicitly teach how to plan, organize, and manage time for the task—and show how it can help the community. Provide scaffolding necessary for understanding and for success.	Metacognitive system—Model procedural self-talk.	Create and use rubrics that are specific. Give heuristics in writing. Provide examples and nonexamples of acceptable work.	Verbalization +46 percentile points Activating prior knowledge +46 percentile points

(Continued)

Instructional Need	Differentiating Context in a Culturally Responsive Classroom	Differentiating Process for Systems of Thinking (Self, Metacognitive, Cognitive)	Differentiating Content and Product	Research-Based Instructional Strategies
To provide locus of control to students	Provide opportunities to lead (such as griot in African American cultures, KIVA). Provide voices and choices in how learning tasks will be accomplished. Visually represent the accomplishment of small tasks in a large project.	Self system—Show belief that students can succeed; mirror assets that they bring to the task. Metacognitive system—Explicitly teach goal-setting; assist with setting realistic timelines and means to measure accomplishment of tasks, especially with complex tasks; give praise for small steps, good decision-making, and problem-solving.	Provide scaffolding for the tasks assigned, and slowly remove the scaffolding as students can handle the tasks on their own.	Teaching for relevancy +40 percentile points Goal-setting with realistic timelines +39 percentile points
To teach cause/effect	Directly teach cause and effect in the classroom using small groups with nonlinguistic organizers to record the thinking. Point out that for every action there is a reaction in both academics and behavior. Provide practice on issues relevant to their culture. Use the KIVA process.	Cognitive system—Provide explicit instruction in knowledge utilization processes like solving problems, conducting an inquiry, making decisions, and conducting investigations; provide explicit instruction and tools for students to record the results of information processing strategies such as cause and effect, comparing and contrasting, categorizing, making inferences, and so on.	Use visual, graphic representations to show the patterns between new learning and known learning. Provide the heuristics for successfully achieving quality products, and provide choices in how students will demonstrate their learning that are relevant to their condition.	Graphic representations +49 percentile points Compare and contrast +40 percentile points Heuristics +38 percentile points Synectics +45 percentile points Concept attainment +41 percentile points Manipulatives +31 percentile points Model-making +31 percentile points Critical thinking skills +41 percentile points

(Continued)

Instructional Need	Differentiating Context in a Culturally Responsive Classroom	Differentiating Process for Systems of Thinking (Self, Metacognitive, Cognitive)	Differentiating Content and Product	Research-Based Instructional Strategies
To teach prioritizing	Directly teach students to plan and sequence a task. Make the learning personally relevant. Help provide meaning to the content by making that content culturally relevant. Directly teach decision-making. Show students that they have a variety of choices for actions and decisions.	Metacognitive system—Model procedural self-talk. Encourage goal-setting by students. Provide opportunities to problem-solve and set priorities.	Use contracts that specify steps and dates that the steps will be completed.	Verbalization *+46 percentile points* Goal-setting *+39 percentile points* Myers-Briggs problem-solving Problem-solving using the Six Hats
To develop trust in people/ systems	Help students to learn to work through systems to achieve their goals. Be cognizant that parents and their children often do not trust systems —and know why. Demonstrate that you care about them, believe that they can learn, and won't give up—no matter what. Welcome students personally every day. Use affirmations.	Self system—Mirror assets that students bring to the task; praise effort. Provide opportunities for students to self-evaluate themselves on learning tasks based on written rubrics provided ahead of time that define quality work (with examples). Provide opportunities for students to work in groups and to receive feedback from peers (transfer trust from peer to group to class to school).	Build and model trust through getting rid of the "gotchas;" provide a rubric that specifies what students must do to be successful on their processes and the point value for the essential elements.	Praising effort *+29 percentile points* Teach and assess students' ability to demonstrate empathy. Cooperative groups *+28 percentile points*

(Continued)

Instructional Need	Differentiating Context in a Culturally Responsive Classroom	Differentiating Process for Systems of Thinking (Self, Metacognitive, Cognitive)	Differentiating Content and Product	Research-Based Instructional Strategies
To show that effort, not luck, will result in achievement	Understand where this concept is originating and guide students to understand cause and effect; specifically point out occurrences where they overcome difficulty by effort in their cultural context. Directly teach students that there are choices for actions. Teach students decision-making skills. Use affirmations. Provide opportunities to lead in small groups. Use the KIVA process.	Metacognitive system—Provide a clear map for accomplishing a task. Cognitive system—Assist in helping children in selecting effective strategies for learning, monitoring their learning, and gauging whether the strategies they've chosen to accomplish their goals are working for them or not.	Help students understand complexity rather than difficulty. Use a step-by-step contract that shows interval successes based on effort.	*Praising effort + 29 percentile points* *Disposition monitoring +33 percentile points*

(Continued)

174

Instructional Need	Differentiating Context in a Culturally Responsive Classroom	Differentiating Process for Systems of Thinking (Self, Metacognitive, Cognitive)	Differentiating Content and Product	Research-Based Instructional Strategies
To increase students' expectations of schooling	Directly tell students and help them understand how the learning is personally relevant. Explicitly teach the value system of the dominant culture, and at the same time, provide ways for students to learn that meet the cultural needs from family and community (collectivist). Involve parents and community in the learning process; take time to learn the culture represented by parents and community.	Self system—When presenting a learning task, address the connections to students' personal lives (including culture) for relevancy. Metacognitive system—Assist students in monitoring their accomplishments; provide a visual representation of their success.	Use a contract with interval goals.	Goal-setting +39 percentile points Teaching for relevancy +40 percentile points Disposition monitoring +33 percentile points
To teach an appropriate response to criticism and authority	Directly teach cause and effect in behavior. Provide criticism in private so as not to shame, and be responsive to the cultural responses to criticism (especially for Mexican Americans). Understand the culture so that the way in which students are disciplined is understood (in some cultures it is important to look students directly in the eye; in others that is an insult). Directly provide choices and guide students through the kinds of choices that they have in reactions.	Self system—Explicitly teach social skills that may not be known (such as taking no for an answer, asking for what you need to learn, delivering a sincere apology, recognizing criticism may be for the behavior and not the person); provide constructive criticism privately and not in front of peers so as not to shut down the cognitive system while the affective takes over.	Use a rubric that is specific to measure not only success but quality. Use a contract that includes feedback throughout the process.	

(Continued)

instructional Need	Differentiating Context in a Culturally Responsive Classroom	Differentiating Process for Systems of Thinking (Self, Metacognitive, Cognitive)	Differentiating Content and Product	Research-Based Instructional Strategies
To provide support systems	Understand the various support systems in the community. Engage community groups to participate in the classroom (such as neighborhood anti-gang advocates). Give voice and choices in learning tasks. Provide opportunities for students to help each other in the classroom.	Metacognitive system—Use self-evaluation rubrics.	Help students to see the system used in creating quality products and how each step affects the final result.	
To increase vocabulary and background knowledge for a learning task	Always teach the vocabulary of the lessons before beginning instruction where it is needed. Provide nonlinguistic ways for students to demonstrate learning. Find ways for students who have acquired background knowledge in a different way to express that knowledge.	Cognitive system—Preteach vocabulary with students creating nonlinguistic representations of terminology; use music, pictures, art, dance, movement, and symbols to help students learn new words and be able to build crystallized intelligence to express background knowledge.		Vocabulary strategies *+49 percentile points*

(Continued)

Instructional Need	Differentiating Context in a Culturally Responsive Classroom	Differentiating Process for Systems of Thinking (Self, Metacognitive, Cognitive)	Differentiating Content and Product	Research-Based Instructional Strategies
To activate prior knowledge and experience	Use the prior knowledge and experience to build on for understanding the new learning. Provide opportunities for culturally relevant knowledge and experience to be shared even though it might not be what the dominant culture is expecting. Honor the background knowledge of the culture and build on it rather than criticize it.	Metacognitive system—Use all five pathways to store and retrieve memories.	Build on student gifts and interests.	*Activating prior knowledge +46 percentile points*
To make learning relevant	Since culture defines where we focus our attention, attend to the cultures in your classroom to make a learning task personally relevant. Create an inviting, culturally responsive environment to hook students.	Self system—Allow students to be motivated and want to undertake a learning task if the task is relevant to them.	Vary products using frames of reference. Vary the products that students produce based on relevancy, complexity, and Bloom's Taxonomy, and provide scaffolding required for success with all products.	*Teaching for relevancy +40 percentile points*

Table 9-2: Differentiation Steps Rubric

Planning	
• Identify state standards to be addressed in a unit of teaching.	• Plan for choosing instructional strategies that will assist students in meaning-making (relevancy).
• Identify prerequisite skills and knowledge needed, including vocabulary to be pretaught (scaffolding).	• Plan for grouping options.
• Have examples and nonexamples of acceptable work.	• Preassess readiness of students.
• Plan for creating a culturally responsive classroom—contextualize for culture.	• Identify student interests—contextualize.
	• Establish learning profiles.
• Plan for engaging self system (motivation/volition, prior knowledge and experience, personal relevance and meaning).	• Take learning style inventories.
	• Identify auditory, visual, and kinesthetic learners.
• Plan for engaging the metacognitive system (student goal-setting, creating reasonable timelines, choosing approach to learning).	• Plan to address multiple intelligences.
	• Use Bloom's Taxonomy.
• Plan for creating a brain-compatible environment.	• Give learning choices and voices (efficacy; relevancy; relationships; locus of control).
• Plan for teaching the dominant culture of the classroom as well as the culture of the students in the classroom.	
Differentiating Context	
• Create a culturally responsive classroom.	• Provide a variety of ways in which students can learn together, and strengthen acceptance of differences through collaborative groups, circle sharing, four corners, group study, partner groups, think-pair-share, cooperative learning, peer evaluations (relationships).
• Build on student interests.	
• Incorporate student cultural background.	
• Create an inviting classroom environment and materials that reflect the diversity of the classroom (relationships).	• Provide opportunities to problem-solve and set priorities; use KIVA (prioritizing).
• Teach to student modalities.	• Provide opportunities for students to self-evaluate themselves on learning tasks based on written rubrics provided ahead of time that define quality work, with examples (trust).
• Value all types of intelligences (efficacy).	
• Tap into prior learning and background knowledge.	
• Tie prior learning and experiences to the new learning (planning).	• Provide opportunities for students to work in groups and to receive feedback from peers; transfer trust from peer to group to class to school (trust).

(Continued)

Differentiating Content and Product

- Provide adjusted assignments or tiered assignments (planning, prioritizing; effort versus luck; support systems; relevancy).

- Cognitive system—Provide explicit instruction in *knowledge utilization* processes like problem solving, conducting an inquiry, decision-making, and conducting an investigation.

- Provide explicit instruction and tools for students to record the results of *information processing* strategies such as cause and effect, comparing and contrasting, categorizing, making inferences, and so on (relevancy; prior knowledge and experience; effort versus luck; cause and effect; problem solving; efficacy).

- Use visual, graphic representations to show the patterns between new learning and known learning.

- Provide the heuristics for successfully achieving quality products, and provide choices in how students will demonstrate learning in ways that are relevant to their condition (locus of control; efficacy; rigor; relevancy; cause and effect).

- Provide scaffolding for the tasks assigned, and slowly remove the scaffolding as students can handle the tasks on their own (locus of control).

- Use tools that develop metacognitive learning (graphic organizers like KWL) that identify what you know and what you don't know or want to learn.

- Talk about thinking or thinking aloud; verbalize the thinking to enhance dual encoding.

- Clarify thinking using paired problem-solving.

- Keep a thinking journal.

- Explicitly teach students to estimate time requirements, organize materials, schedule procedures, and perform self-evaluation.

- Vary products using frames of reference.

- Vary the products that students produce based on relevancy, complexity, and Bloom's Taxonomy, and provide scaffolding required for success with all products (relevancy).

- Start with kids where they are, and move them up the levels of thinking (Bloom's Taxonomy).

- Provide choices.

- Let students choose to work above level, but never below their abilities (efficacy).

Differentiating Process

- Cognitive system—Assist in creating support systems (included in the rubrics) for the tasks within the process of accomplishing the tasks; create self-evaluation rubrics (support systems).

- Provide explicit feedback.

- Use effective instructional strategies that allow students to make meaning of the content (such as Six Thinking Hats, problem-solving strategies, praise for effort, synectics, teaching for relevancy, verbalization, goal-setting, vocabulary strategies, activating prior knowledge, scaffolding, cues, questioning strategies, compare and contrast).

- Provide choice (efficacy); explicitly teach students that we have choices in behavior and decision-making and teach how to make appropriate choices.

- Use flexible grouping options (relationships, support systems, trust, generational expectations of schooling; prior knowledge and experience; relevancy; diversity).

- Self system—Build beliefs that they can achieve as a learner based on assets (efficacy).

- Metacognitive system—Strengthen the ability to set goals and monitor how students are doing with the strategies they've selected to attain the goals (efficacy).

- Metacognitive system—Procedural self-talk (planning)

- Self system—Mirror assets that students bring to the task.

(Continued)

Differentiating Process	
• Metacognitive system—Procedural self-talk (planning) • Self system—Mirror assets that students bring to the task. • Metacognitive system—Explicitly teach goal-setting; assist with setting realistic timelines and means to measure accomplishment of tasks, especially with complex tasks (locus of control, trust). • Self system—Explicitly teach social skills that may not be known (such as taking no for an answer, asking for what you need to learn, delivering a sincere	apology, recognizing criticism may be for behavior not the person); provide constructive criticism privately and not in front of peers so as not to shut down the cognitive system while the affective takes over (response to criticism and authority). • Cognitive system—Preteach vocabulary with students, and create nonlinguistic representations of terminology (vocabulary). • Metacognitive system—Use strategies that use all five pathways to store and retrieve memories (prior experience and knowledge).
Student Evaluations	
• Provide written rubrics that clearly describe the characteristics of quality work for each critical attribute of the assignment so that students can self-evaluate; use peer evaluation (relationships, relevancy, planning, efficacy, locus of control). • Prepare written rubrics that are specific heuristics (grades 2–12). • Provide examples of student work at different levels of performance to assist students in evaluating their own work (efficacy, locus of control, consequences, cause and effect, planning, response to criticism, support systems, relevancy). • Allow students to self-evaluate for each of the steps along the way of a complex project or task.	• Provide consistency; eliminate "gotchas" (relationships, trust, locus of control). • Use explicit feedback often and in a variety of forms including teacher, peer, and self. • Use praise appropriately and in ways that are relevant to cultural and diversity needs; provide praise in a variety of formats including verbal, written, peer-generated, self-generated, and outside-voice generated (by parent or school volunteer, for example). • Use early intervention no matter the age of the student (intervention at the point of detection). • Provide a variety of intervention strategies based on culture, age, and background knowledge. • Involve caregivers, community resources, and school resources.

Afterword

By Rosilyn Carroll

As a lifelong learner and educator who has been waiting impatiently for a book that provides a careful academic and cultural examination of what works for poor children and children of color, I am happy to see this book by Donna Walker Tileston and Sandra Darling, which addresses both issues in a clear and useful manner.

Today the schools in North America are becoming more and more culturally diverse, filled with students whose home language is not English, and with students who are eligible for free or reduced lunch. Yet most of the instruction, curriculum, assessment, and teacher preparation training are aimed at white, middle-class students who speak only English. Most educational publishers' curriculum is still geared to this group as well, even though they have shaded in the skin color of the students on the book covers, changed some of the fictitious students' names to reflect cultural diversity, and added a few culturally diverse entries in the recommended reading lists and references.

Higher education institutions have done even less to address economic, cultural, and linguistic diversity in teacher preparation. There may be a course here and there or a mention of diverse issues in a standard course, but faculty discussions still tiptoe around topics of race, culture, and poverty as if they were not relevant to education. First-year teachers continuously tell me that they are not prepared to adequately teach poor students or students of color. This work by Tileston and Darling is important because it addresses these vital but much-neglected areas of teacher education. Although not specifically written for English-language learners, I believe the processes described in this publication will also work for them.

Why Culture Counts: Teaching Children of Poverty will assist new and senior teachers in facilitating the learning process of children and youth who, for over 100 years, have been overlooked, misdiagnosed, and—some would say—not cared about. Finally, we as educators have a text that confronts how to differentiate instruction that will make an academic difference for children of poverty and students of color.

Why Culture Counts opens with a comment by Dr. Belinda Williams that our current models do not address the complexity of achievement gaps among racial and socioeconomic groups; these models are missing the significant implications of culture and race, and they are missing an integrated discussion that will address human development in varied cultural contexts.

If we are to teach children and youth and they are to successfully learn at or above grade level, we must see not only the similarities but also the differences in our students. By differences, in this context, I don't mean individual differences or uniqueness, but *group* differences. We must see and understand, without negative judgments, that our students come to us with culture, and that culture is a group (not an individual) phenomenon.

Which has greater impact on student achievement, poverty or culture? As the authors have written elsewhere, "If we take the variable of poverty out of the achievement gap equation, children of color who are middle-class or affluent still score lower than white middle-class students. This merely reinforces that race in U.S. schools impacts the achievement of students of color except Asian students (Hmong students not included)" (Mangaliman, 2007, p. 1). Students of color and white students bring cultural attributes to the classroom that are often overlooked. Some teachers, more than I care to say, will state that they do not see the color or culture of their students.

In fact, many teachers believe these students "do not have culture." The late John Ogbu, a noted educational anthropologist formerly at Berkeley, referred to this failure to perceive color or culture in schools as *cultural discontinuity* in the schooling experience.

One effect of cultural discontinuity is that some teachers tend to view *all* their students as culturally white, and when they do not respond like white students, regard them as less intelligent, or in need of being fixed, or as behavior problems who are "hard to teach."

A hidden aspect of cultural discontinuity is that many educational institutions tend to value only European Anglo-Saxon culture. By not allowing the cultures of students of color to be an integral part of the school environment, schools are requiring these students to enter a cultural environment that, for them, is unhealthy. Thus, while white students enter school and concentrate on academics, students of color must concentrate on learning the "school culture" so that they can fit in. Since students of color must also learn the academic information, this cultural discontinuity becomes one of the causes of the achievement gap. In other words, while children may come into school with an achievement gap, it actually grows while they are there. We must strive to overcome poverty and colorblindness. When we impose our mistaken belief that students of color or poor children have the same values, beliefs, world views, and customs as white middle-class students living in the United States, the teacher is setting poor students and students of color up for failure.

Why Culture Counts stresses that teachers must examine their own background knowledge and experiences in dealing with and understanding their own culture and race. This is such an important component in improving student achievement, because without understanding one's own culture and its influence on learning, it is very difficult to understand the impact that students' cultures have on *their* learning.

Finally, *Why Culture Counts* engages in a discussion of human development from a cultural and socioeconomic context. It applies practical, research-based strategies that work for white middle-class students, students in poverty, and students of color. If schools in the United States used these methods, students' academic growth would be phenomenal—not just students of color and poor students, but all students. When there is an environment of learning, one demonstrating that all students can really achieve beyond mediocrity, then everyone benefits. Differentiating instruction for all students forces the standard to rise: Students find themselves doing more, and teachers find themselves raising the bar and preparing for success. Parents benefit, the community benefits, and the achievement gap closes. There is less crime and there are better cross-cultural relationships and fewer people in jail; economic growth rises, and everyone is prepared to fully participate in this new and wondrous, rapidly changing information age.

Rosilyn M. Carroll *is academic director for the Center for Excellence in Urban Teaching at Hamline University in St. Paul, Minnesota. She has developed pluralistic curricula for groups in Africa, Asia, Mexico, Europe, and the United States.*

References

Mangaliman, J. (2007). Poverty can't explain racial, ethnic divide. *Mercury News.* Accessed at www.mercurynews.com on August 16, 2007.

Williams, B. (Ed.). *Closing the achievement gap: A vision for changing beliefs and practices* (2nd ed.). Alexandria, VA: Association for Supervision and Curriculum Development.

References

Ackerman, P. L. (1996). A theory of adult intellectual development: Process, personality, interests, and knowledge. *Intelligence, 22,* 227–257.

African-American Voices in Children's Fiction. (2007). Compiled by Arrowhead Library System. Accessed at http://als.lib.wi.us/AACList.html on October 20, 2007.

Alva, S. A. (1991). Academic invulnerability among Mexican-American students: The importance of protective resources and appraisals. *Hispanic Journal of Behavioral Sciences, 13,* 18–34.

Banks, J. A. (2001). *Cultural diversity and education.* Boston: Allyn & Bacon.

Barakat, H. (1993). *The Arab world: Society, culture, and state.* London: University of California Press.

Benard, B. (1996). Fostering resiliency in urban schools. In B. Williams (Ed.), *Closing the achievement gap: A vision for changing beliefs and practices* (1st ed., pp. 96–119). Alexandria, VA: Association for Supervision and Curriculum Development.

Benard, B. (1997). *Turning it around for all youth: From risk to resilience.* New York: ERIC Clearinghouse on Urban Education. (ERIC/CUE Digest No. 126).

Benard, B. (2003). Turnaround teachers and schools. In B. Williams (Ed.), *Closing the achievement gap: A vision for changing beliefs and practices* (2nd ed., pp.115–137). Alexandria, VA: Association for Supervision and Curriculum Development.

Bianchi, J. (1991). *Snowed In at Pokeweed Public School.* Buffalo, NY: Firefly Books.

Bibliography of Children's Literature Focusing on Latino People, History, and Culture. (2007). Accessed at http://clnet.ucla.edu/Latino_Bibliography.html on October 20, 2007.

Blake, I. K. (1993). Learning language in context: The social-emotional orientation of African American mother-child communication. *International Journal of Behavioral Development, 16*(3), 443–464.

Blake, I. K. (1994). Language development and socialization in young African-American children. In P. M. Greenfield & R. R. Cocking (Eds.), *Cross-cultural roots of minority child development* (pp. 167–195). Hillsdale, NJ: Lawrence Erlbaum Associates.

Bloom, B. S. (Ed.). (1956). Taxonomy of Educational Objectives: The classification of educational goals. Handbook I: *Cognitive Domain.* New York: McKay.

Bloom, B. S. (1984a). *Taxonomy of educational objectives.* Boston: Allyn & Bacon.

Bloom, B. S. (1984b). The 2 Sigma problem: The search for methods of instruction as effective as one-to-one tutoring. *Educational Researcher, 13*(6), 4–16.

Bloom, B. S. (1984c). The search for methods of group instruction as effective as one-to-one tutoring. *Educational Leadership, 41*(8), 4–18.

Brophy, J. E. (1982). Successful teaching strategies for the inner city child. *Phi Delta Kappan, 64,* 527–530.

Carol, L. N. (1993). KIVA: A leadership initiative and technique. In L. Gray (Ed.), *Leadership: Preparing leaders for changing schools* (pp. 18–20). St. Paul, MN: Minnesota Association of School Administrators.

Carroll, R. (2001). Embedding of the Urban Learner Framework in the online course, Teaching for Relevancy. Chandler, AZ: Learning Bridges.

Chappuis, S., & Chappuis, J. (December 2007/January 2008). The best value in formative assessment. *Educational Leadership, 65*(4), 14–18.

Chomsky, N. (1957). *Syntactic structures.* The Hague: Mouton.

Chomsky, N. (1965). *Aspects of a theory of syntax.* Cambridge, MA: MIT Press.

Cole, R. (Ed.). (1995). *Educating everybody's children.* Alexandria, VA: Association for Supervision and Curriculum Development.

Commission on Chapter 1. (1992). *Making schools work for children in poverty.* Washington, DC: American Association for Higher Education.

Daniels, L. A. (Ed.). (2002). *The state of Black America 2002.* New York: National Urban League.

Darling, S. (1999). *Aligned instructional database.* Chandler, AZ: Learning Bridges.

Darling-Hammond, L. (2000, January 1). Teacher quality and student achievement: A review of state policy and evidence. *Education Policy Analysis Archives, 8*(1). Accessed at http://epaa.asu.edu/epaa/v8n1 on May 19, 2008.

Darling-Hammond, L., & Post, L. (2000). Inequality in teaching and schooling: Supporting high-quality teaching and leadership in low-income schools. In R. D. Kalenberg (Ed.), *A nation at risk: Preserving public education as an engine for social mobility* (pp. 127–165). New York: Century Foundation Press.

Delgado-Gaitan, C. (1993). Parenting in two generations of Mexican American families. *International Journal of Behavioral Development, 16*(3), 409–427.

de Bono, E. (1999). *Six thinking hats.* Boston: Back Bay Books.

Delgado-Gaitan, C. (1994). Socializing young children in Mexican American families: An intergenerational perspective. In P. M. Greenfield & R. R. Cocking (Eds.), *Cross-cultural roots of minority child development* (pp. 55–86). Hillsdale, NJ: Lawrence Erlbaum Associates.

Dochy, F., Segers, M., & Buehl, M. M. (1999). The relationship between assessment practices and outcomes of studies: The case of research on prior knowledge. *Review of Educational Research, 69*(2), 145–186.

Doty, G. (2007). *Classroom assessment and data analysis.* Online course. Chandler, AZ: Learning Bridges.

Feuerstein, R. (1980). *Instrumental enrichment: An intervention program for cognitive modifiability.* Glenview, IL: Scott Foresman.

Fraser, B. J., Walberg, H. J., Welch, W. W., & Hattie, J. A. (1987). Synthesis of educational productivity research. *Journal of Educational Research, 11*(2), 145–252.

Friedman, T. L. (2005). *The world is flat: A brief history of the twenty-first century.* New York: Farrar, Straus and Giroux.

Gardner, H. (1993). *Frames of mind: The theory of multiple intelligences* (2nd ed.) London: Fontana.

Gardner, H. (1999). *Intelligence reframed: Multiple intelligences for the 21st century.* New York: Basic Books.

Garmezy, N. (1991). Resiliency and vulnerability to adverse developmental outcomes associated with poverty. *American Behavioral Scientist, 34*(4), 416–430.

Gay, G. (2000). *Culturally responsive teaching: Theory, research, and practice.* Multicultural Education Series. New York: Teachers College Press.

Gay, G. (2002). Preparing for culturally responsive teaching. *Journal of Teacher Education, 4*(2), 106–116.

Gewertz, C. (2007). High-achieving students in low-income families said likely to fall behind. *Education Week.* Accessed at www.edweek.org on September 18, 2007.

Gonzales, R., & Padilla, A. M. (1997). The academic resilience of Mexican American high school students. *Hispanic Journal of Behavioral Sciences, 19,* 301–317.

Good, T. L. (1983). Recent classroom research: Implications for teacher education. In D. C. Smith (Ed.), *Essential knowledge for beginning educators* (pp. 1–10). Washington, DC: American Association of Colleges for Teacher Education.

Goodrich, A. H. (2000). Using rubrics to promote thinking and learning. *Educational Learning, 57*(5), 2, 13–18.

Greenfield, P. M. (1984). A theory of the teacher in the learning activities of everyday life. In B. Rogoff & J. Lave (Eds.), *Everyday cognition: Its development in social context* (pp. 117–138). Cambridge, MA: Harvard University Press.

Greenfield, P. M. (1994). Independence and interdependence as developmental script: Implications for theory, research, and practice. In P. M. Greenfield & R. R. Cocking (Eds.), *Cross-cultural roots of minority child development* (pp. 1–37). Hillsdale, NJ: Lawrence Erlbaum Associates.

Greenfield, P. M., Brazelton, T. B., & Childs, C. (1989). From birth to maturity in Zinacantan: Ontogenesis in cultural context. In V. Bricker & G. Gossen (Eds.), *Ethnographic encounters in Southern Meso-america: Celebrating essays in honor of Evon Z. Vogt* (pp. 177–216). Albany, NY: Institute of Mesoamerican Studies, State University of New York.

Greenfield, P. M., & Cocking, R. R. (Eds.). (1994). *Cross-cultural roots of minority child development.* Hillsdale, NJ: Lawrence Erlbaum Associates.

Haberman, M. (1991). The pedagogy of poverty versus good teaching. *Phi Delta Kappan, 73,* 290–294.

Haberman, M. (2005). *Star teachers of children in poverty.* Indianapolis, IN: Kappa Delta Pi.

Harden, B. (2006, June 22). From 1970 to 2000, metro areas showed widening gap between rich, poor sections. *The Washington Post,* p. A03.

Henderson, N., & Milstein, M. M. (1996). *Resiliency in schools: Making it happen for students and educators.* Thousand Oaks, CA: Corwin Press.

Hetherington, E. M., Cox, M., & Cox, R. (1982). Effects of divorce on parents and children. In M. Lamb (Ed.), *Nontraditional families.* Hillsdale, NJ: Lawrence Erlbaum Associates.

Hofstede, G. (1983). National cultures revisited. *Behavior Science Revisited, 18,* 285–305.

Jensen, E. (1997). *Completing the puzzle.* Del Mar, CA: The Brain Store.

Jensen, E. (2004). The brain and learning. Dallas, TX: Workshop.

Jones, S. J. (2003). *Blueprint for student success.* Thousand Oaks, CA: Corwin Press.

Joyce, B., & Weil, M. (2000). *Models of teaching* (6th ed.). Needham Heights, MA: Allyn & Bacon.

Kagan, S., & Zahn, G. L. (1975). Field dependence and the school achievement gap between Anglo-American and Mexican-American children. *Journal of Educational Psychology, 67,* 643–650.

Kim, U., & Choi, S. H. (1994). Individualism, collectivism, and child development: A Korean perspective. In P. M. Greenfield & R. R. Cocking (Eds.), *Cross-cultural roots of minority child development* (pp. 226–258). Hillsdale, NJ: Lawrence Erlbaum Associates.

Kunjufu, J. (2002). *Black students, middle class teachers.* Chicago, IL: African American Images.

Kunjufu, J. (2005a). *Hip hop street curriculum.* Saulk Village, IL: African American Images.

Kunjufu, J. (2005b). *Keeping black boys out of special education.* Chicago, IL: African American Images.

Kunjufu, J. (2006). *An African centered response to Ruby Payne's poverty theory.* Chicago, IL: African American Images.

Laczko-Kerr, I., & Berliner, D. (2003). In harm's way: How undercertified teachers hurt their students. *Educational Leadership, 60,* 8.

Ladson-Billings, G. (1994). *The dreamkeepers: Successful teachers of African American children.* San Francisco: Jossey-Bass.

Lavoie, R. D. (1996). *Understanding learning disabilities: How difficult can this be? The F.A.T. city workshop* [Video]. Washington, DC: Public Broadcasting System.

Lebra, T. S. (1994). Mother and child in a Japanese socialization: A Japan-U.S. comparison. In P. M. Greenfield & R. R. Cocking (Eds.), *Cross-cultural roots of minority child development* (pp. 259–274). Hillsdale, NJ: Lawrence Erlbaum Associates.

Mangaliman, J. (2007). Poverty can't explain racial, ethnic divide. *Mercury News.* Accessed at mercurynews.com on August 16, 2007.

Manning, J. B., & Kovach, J. (2003). The continuing challenges of excellence and equity. In B. Williams (Ed.), *Closing the achievement gap: A vision for changing beliefs and practices* (2nd ed., pp. 25–47). Alexandria, VA: Association for Supervision and Curriculum Development.

Markus, H. R., & Kitayama, S. (1991). Culture and the self: Implications for cognition, emotion, and motivation. *Psychological Review, 98*(2), 242–253.

Marzano, R. (1998). *A theory-based meta-analysis of research on instruction.* Aurora, CO: Mid-continent Research for Education and Learning.

Marzano, R. (2003). Direct vocabulary instruction: An idea whose time has come. In B. Williams (ed.), *Closing the achievement gap: A vision for changing beliefs and practices* (2nd ed., pp. 48–66). Alexandria, VA: Association for Supervision and Curriculum Development.

Marzano, R., & Kendall, J. (1996). *Designing standards-based district, schools, and classrooms.* Alexandria, VA: Association for Supervision and Curriculum Development.

Maston, A. (1994). Resilience in individual development: Successful adaptation despite risk and adversity. In M. Wang & E. Gordon (Eds.), *Educational resilience in inner-city America: Challenges and prospects.* Hillsdale, NJ: Lawrence Erlbaum Associates.

McCord, C., & Freeman, H. P. (1990). Excess mortality in Harlem. *New England Journal of Medicine, 3,* 322, 173–177.

McKinney, S., Flenner C., Frazier, W., & Abrams, L. (2006). *Responding to the needs of at-risk students in poverty.* Accessed at www.usca.edu/essays/V01172006/mckinney.pdf on September 15, 2007.

McMillan, J. H., & Reed, D. F. (1994). At-risk students and resiliency: Factors contributing to academic success. *The Clearing House, 67,* 137–140.

Morgan, H. (1990). Assessment of students' behavioral interactions during on-task classroom activities. *Perceptual and Motor Skills, 70,* 563–569.

Myers, I. (1980). *Gifts' differing.* Palo Alto, CA: Consulting Psychologists Press.

Myers, I. B., & McCaulley, M. H. (1987). *Manual: A guide to the development and use of the Myers-Briggs Type Indicator.* Palo Alto, CA: Consulting Psychologists Press.

Nagy, W. E., & Herman, P. A. (1984). *Limitations of vocabulary instruction* (Tech. Rep. No. 326). Urbana: University of Illinois, Center for the Study of Reading. (ERIC Document Reproduction Service No. ED 248 498).

National Reading Panel. (2000, April). *Teaching Children to Read.* Accessed at www.nationalreadingpanel.org/ Publications/publications.html on November 12, 2007.

O'Connell, J. (2008). *State of education address.* Accessed at www.cde. ca.gov/eo/in/se/yr08stateofed.asp on May 16, 2008.

Ohanian, S. (2001). News from the test resistance trail. *Phi Delta Kappan, 82*(5), 363–366.

O'Tuel, F. S., and Bullard, R. K. (1993). *Developing higher order thinking in the content areas K–12.* Pacific Grove, CA: Critical Thinking Press.

Pasteur, A. B., & Toldson, I. L. (1982). *Roots of soul: The psychology of black expressiveness.* Garden City, NY: Anchor Press/Doubleday.

Payne, R. K. (2001). *A framework for understanding poverty.* Highlands, TX: Aha Press.

Pink, D. (2005). *A whole new mind: Moving from the information age to the conceptual age.* New York: Riverhead Books.

Popham, W. J. (2002). Preparing for the coming avalanche of accountability tests. *Harvard Education Letters,* May/June, pp. 9–15.

Popham, W. (2008). *Transformative assessment.* Alexandria, VA: Association for Supervision and Curriculum Development.

Quality Counts. (2006). *Education Week, 25*(17), 8–76.

Quiroz, B., Greenfield, P. M., & Altchech, M. (1999, April). Bridging cultures with a parent-teacher conference. *Educational Leadership, 56*(7), 64–67.

Raeff, C., Greenfield, P. M., & Quiroz, B. (2000). Conceptualizing interpersonal relationships in the cultural contexts of individualism and collectivism. *New Directions in Child and Adolescent Development, 87,* 59–74.

Ramirez, M., & Castenada, A. (1974). *Cultural democracy, bicognitive development, and education.* San Diego, CA: Academic Press.

Rank, M. R. (2005). *One nation, underprivileged.* New York: Oxford University Press.

Reading Graphic Organizers and Printables. (2008). Accessed at www. sanchezclass.com/reading-graphic-organizers.htm on April 15, 2008.

Robinson, B., Shade, C., & Oberg, M. (2000). *Creating culturally responsive classrooms.* Washington, DC: American Psychological Association.

Rolfhus, E. L., & Ackerman, P. L. (1999). Assessing individual differences in knowledge: Knowledge structures and traits. *Journal of Educational Psychology, 91*, 511–526.

Rothstein-Fisch, C., & Trumbull, E. (2008). *Managing diverse classrooms.* Alexandria, VA: Association for Supervision and Curriculum Development.

Rothstein-Fisch, C., Trumbull, E., Isaac, A., Daley, C., & Pérez, A. (2003). When "helping someone else" is the right answer: Teachers bridge cultures in assessment. *Journal of Latinos and Education, 2*(3), 123–140.

Roy, S. (2000). *Graphic representations.* Chandler, AZ: Learning Bridges.

Ruble, D. N., & Nakamura, C. Y. (1972). Task versus social orientation in young children and their attention to relevant social cues. *Child Development, 43,* 471–480.

Rutter, M. (1985). Resilience in the face of adversity: Protective factors and resistance to psychiatric disorder. *British Journal of Psychiatry, 147,* 598–611.

Rychlak, J. (1975). Affective assessment, intelligence, social class and racial learning style. *Journal of Personality and Social Psychology, 32,* 989–995.

Sanchez, M. (2008). Plot and Conflict Analysis and Story Map. Accessed at www.sanchezclass.com/reading-graphic-organizers.htm on June 9, 2008.

Shade, B. (1994). Understanding the African American learner. In E. R. Hollins, J. E. King, & W. C. Hayman (Eds.), *Teaching diverse populations: Formulating a new knowledge base* (pp. 175–189). Albany: State University of New York Press.

Shade, B. J., Kelly, C., & Oberg, M. (1997). *Creating culturally responsive classrooms.* Washington, D.C.: American Psychological Association.

Shade, L. (1993, August). Gender issues in computer networking. Paper presented at Community Networking: The International Free-Net Conference, Ottawa, Canada.

Small, M. (1998). *Our babies, ourselves: How biology and culture shape the way we parent.* New York: Anchor Books.

Sousa, D. A. (2005). *How the brain learns to read.* Thousand Oaks, CA: Corwin Press.

Spangler, D. (2001). Teaching for relevancy. Online course. Chandler, AZ: Learning Bridges.

Stephenson, R. B., & Ellsworth, J. (1993). Dropouts and the silencing of critical voices. In L. Weis & M. Fine (Eds), *Beyond silenced voices: Class, race, and gender in United States Schools* (pp. 259–273). Albany: State University of New York Press.

Stiggins, R. J. (1997). *Student-centered classroom assessment* (2nd Ed.). Upper Saddle River, NJ: Merrill.

Suina, J. H., & Smolkin, L. B. (1994). From natal culture to school culture to dominant society culture: Supporting transitions for Pueblo Indian students. In P. M. Greenfield & R. R. Cocking (Eds.), *Cross-cultural roots of minority child development* (pp. 115–130). Hillsdale, NJ: Lawrence Erlbaum Associates.

Tileston, D. W. (2004a). *What every teacher should know about diverse learners.* Thousand Oaks, CA: Corwin Press.

Tileston, D. W. (2004b).*What every teacher should know about learning, memory and the brain.* Thousand Oaks, CA: Corwin Press.

Tileston, D. W. (2004c). *What every teacher should know about special learners.* Thousand Oaks, CA: Corwin Press.

Tileston, D. W. (2004d). *What every teacher should know about student motivation.* Thousand Oaks, CA: Corwin Press.

Tomlinson, C. A. (1999). *The differentiated classroom: Responding to the needs of all learners.* Alexandria, VA: Association for Supervision and Curriculum Development.

Tomlinson, C. A. (2000). Differentiation of instruction in the elementary grades (Report no. ED0-PS-00-7). Marion, IN: Indiana Wesleyan Center for Educational Excellence. (ERIC Document Reproduction Service No. ED443572). Accessed from EBSCOHost ERIC database September 28, 2007.

Tomlinson, C. (December 2007/January 2008). Learning to love assessment. *Educational Leadership, 65* (4), 8–13.

Triandis, H. C. (1990). Cross-cultural studies of individualism and collectivism. In J. J. Berman (Ed.), *Culture, style and the educative process* (2nd ed., pp. 21, 135). Springfield, IL: Charles C. Thomas.

Trumbull, E. (2005). Language, culture, and society. In E. Trumbull & B. Farr, *Language and learning: What teachers need to know* (pp. 33–72). Norwood, MA: Christopher-Gordon.

Trumbull, E., Diaz-Meza, R., Hasan, A., & Rothstein-Fisch, C. (2001). *The Bridging Cultures Project five-year report, 1996–2000.* Accessed at www.wested.org/bridging/BC_5yr_report.pdf on July 15, 2007.

U.S. Census Bureau. (2006). *Income, poverty, and health insurance coverage in the United States: 2005.* Accessed at www.census.gov/prod/2006pubs/p60–231.pdf on May 23, 2008.

Valencia, R. R. (Ed.). (1991). *Chicano school failure and success: Research and policy agendas for the 1990s.* London: Falmer Press.

Villegas, A. M. (1991). *Culturally responsive pedagogy for the 1990s and beyond.* Princeton, NJ: Educational Testing Service.

Walberg, H. J. (1984). Improving the productivity of America's schools. *Educational Leadership, 41*(8), 19–27.

Wang, M. C., & Kovach, J. A. (1996). *Bridging the achievement gap in urban schools: Reducing educational segregation and advancing resilience-promoting strategies.* Alexandria, VA: Association for Supervision and Curriculum Development.

Wang, M. C., & Reynolds, M. C. (1997). Progressive inclusion: Meeting new challenges in special education. Publication Series No. 3. Philadelphia: Temple University.

Waxman, H., Gray, J., & Padron, Y. (2003). *Review of research on educational resilience.* Berkeley, CA: University of California, Center for Research on Education, Diversity, and Excellence.

Waxman, H. C., & Huang, S. L. (1996). Motivation and learning environment differences between resilient and nonresilient inner-city middle school students. *Journal of Educational Research, 90,* 93–102.

Waxman, H. C., Padron, Y. N., & Arnold, K. A. (2001). Effective instructional practices for students placed at risk of failure. In G. D. Borman, S. C. Stringfield, & R. E. Slavin (Eds.), *Title I: Compensatory education at the crossroads* (pp. 137–70). Accessed at http://repositories.cdlib.org/crede/rsrchrpts/rr-11 on September 15, 2007.

Weinstein, C., Curran, M., & Tomlinson-Clarke, S. (2004). Culturally responsive classroom management. *Journal of Teacher Education, 55*(1), 25–38.

Wenglinsky, H. (2002, February 13). How schools matter: The link between teacher classroom practices and student academic performance. *Education Policy Analysis Archives, 10*(12). Accessed at http://epaa.asu.edu/epaa/v10n12/ on May 5, 2008.

Wereschagin, M. (2007). Pittsburgh study: Teachers key in affecting pupils' success. *Pittsburgh Tribune-Review.* Accessed at www.pittsburghlive.com/ x/pittsburghtrib/?source=network+bar on September 11, 2007.

Werner, E. E., & Smith, R. S. (1992). *Overcoming the odds: High risk children from birth to adulthood.* Ithaca, NY: Cornell University Press.

Wiggins, G., & McTighe, J. (2001). *Understanding by design.* New York: Prentice Hall.

Wiggins, G., & McTighe, J. (2005). *Understanding by design* (2nd ed). New York: Prentice Hall.

Williams, B. (1996). *Closing the achievement gap: A vision for changing beliefs and practices.* Alexandria, VA: Association for Supervision and Curriculum Development.

Williams, B. (2003). *Closing the achievement gap: A vision for changing beliefs and practices* (2nd ed.). Alexandria, VA. Association for Supervision and Curriculum Development.

Zeichner, K. (2003). Pedagogy, knowledge, and teacher preparation. In B. Williams (Ed.), *Closing the achievement gap: A vision for changing beliefs and practices* (2nd ed., pp. 99–114). Alexandria, VA: Association for Supervision and Curriculum Development.

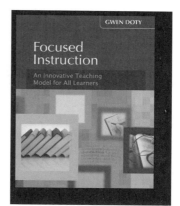

Total Instructional Alignment:
From Standards to Student Success
Lisa Carter
Replace an antiquated education system
with a flexible, proactive one that ensures
learning for all by focusing on three
important domains of the alignment
process.　　　　　　　　　　**BKF222**

Focused Instruction: An Innovative
Teaching Model for All Learners
Gwen Doty
Effectively respond to diverse learning
styles and achievement levels with
strategies and reproducible tools that help
you customize, scaffold, and layer your
instruction.　　　　　　　　　　**BKF249**

The Kids Left Behind: Catching Up the
Underachieving Children of Poverty
Robert Barr, William Parrett
Successfully reach and teach the
underachieving children of poverty with
the help of this comprehensive resource.
　　　　　　　　　　BKF216

Reclaiming Youth At Risk:
Our Hope for the Future
Larry K. Brendtro, Martin Brokenleg, and
Steve Van Bockern
Venture inside schools that have
successfully reached youth at risk. Set
includes three 20-minute DVDs and a
facilitator's guide.　　　　　　　**DVF011**

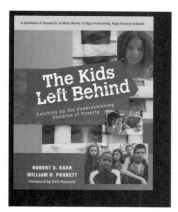

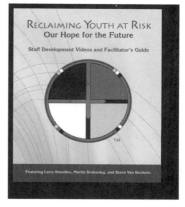

Solution Tree | Press
a division of
Solution Tree

Visit solution-tree.com or call 800.733.6786 to order.